PRIESTLY CELIBACY

ITS SCRIPTURAL, HISTORICAL, SPIRITUAL, AND PSYCHOLOGICAL ROOTS

PRIESTLY CELIBACY
Its Scriptural, Historical, Spiritual, and Psychological Roots

EDITED BY REVEREND PETER M. J. STRAVINSKAS

NEWMAN HOUSE PRESS

ADDRESS CORRESPONDENCE TO:
Editor, Newman House, 21 Fairview Avenue, Mt. Pocono, PA 18344

ISBN 0–9704022–2–8

COVER ART:
Crucifixion, from a Missal, Germany (Abbey of Weingarten),
c. 1200–1232. M.710, f. 10v.
The Pierpont Morgan Library / Art Resource, N.Y.

COVER DESIGN: Paul Zomberg
COMPOSITION: Shoreline Graphics, Rockland, Maine

Text composed in Stempel Garamond 11/14

Printed in the United States of America

CONTENTS

Introduction, *by Rev. Peter M. J. Stravinskas*   7

Preface, *by Kenneth J. Howell*   9

KENNETH J. HOWELL
The Teaching of Christ on Priestly Celibacy   13

REVEREND RAY RYLAND
A Brief History of Clerical Celibacy   27

REVEREND PETER M. J. STRAVINSKAS
Celibacy and the Meaning of the Priesthood   45

JOHN HAAS
Marriage and the Priesthood   64

REVEREND DAVID HARTMAN
Why I'm Not a Celibate—But Glad That Catholic
    Priests Are!   86

JESSICA MILLARD HARTMAN
Clerical Marriage from a Wife's Viewpoint   95

WANDA POLTAWSKA
Priestly Celibacy in the Light of Medicine and
    Psychology   107

APPENDICES

POPE PAUL VI
On the Celibacy of the Priest   125

POPE JOHN PAUL II
The Meaning of Celibacy   169

INTRODUCTION

"We shall not cease from exploration, and the end of all our exploring will be to arrive where we started and know the place for the first time." So wrote T. S. Eliot about the searching for meaning and truth that seems to be the incessant lot of man here below. I think it applies in a striking manner to present-day discussions and studies regarding clerical celibacy, as illustrated not only by this present book but by the fact that its contributors include: a Protestant minister; three former Protestant clergymen, one of whom is now a Catholic priest; two Catholic laymen; and a minister's wife, now herself a Catholic. While Dr. Wanda Poltawska and I are "cradle" Catholics, the other contributors to this volume show that this topic can indeed benefit from a consideration "from the outside."

Much of the discussion regarding clerical celibacy since about 1960 has generated mostly heat, seldom rising above "cheap-advocacy" literature. Of course, the authors represented in the present volume make no claim to neutrality: they are strongly in favor of the tradition—in truth, the apostolic tradition—of priestly celibacy. They have, however, tried to produce a work that is biblically grounded, theologically sound, historically accurate, and eminently rooted in the exigencies of contemporary Catholic life.

As I edited each chapter, I kept before my eyes the dying Christ giving birth to His Church. As St. Augustine puts it so beautifully and poetically: "Here was opened wide the door of life, from which the sacraments of the Church have flowed out, without which there is no entering in unto eternal life which is true life. . . . Here the second Adam with bowed head slept upon the cross, that thence a wife might be formed of Him, flowing from His side while He slept." [1] What is especially striking in Saint John's depiction of that scene is the presence of three virgins, so beautifully and movingly depicted in the thirteenth-century miniature painting reproduced on our cover: the Son of God Himself, His immaculate Mother, and the Beloved Disciple. That sacred conversation gave us the virginal Church to be the Mother of the many brethren of the Savior.

May Jesus, Mary, and John assist all in the Church, but especially the clergy, to achieve a renewed appreciation of how loving and life-giving consecrated celibacy can and should be.

REV. PETER M. J. STRAVINSKAS

---

[1] *In Ioannem*, 117.3.

PREFACE

The requirement of celibacy for priests in the Catholic Church has been under close scrutiny and even heated debate for almost three decades now. Many people in the Church, both clerical and lay, wonder about the necessity and value of retaining this ancient tradition. Many of the problems they perceive in the clergy can be attributed, in their view, to this antiquated practice. Some look to non-Catholic Christian traditions as models for avoiding the problems they see in the Catholic clergy, while others question whether non-married clergy can really address the problems pressing on families in our parishes. On every side, clerical celibacy is being questioned, examined, and debated. This book addresses those questions.

In this book, seven authors argue that there are many solid reasons to retain and promote the discipline of clerical celibacy: biblical, historical, theological, and practical. Because the Catholic Church places unmitigated trust in the Bible as the Word of God, she turns first to Scripture to see what the inspired authors have to teach us. Here, our present authors find celibacy grounded in the teaching of Jesus Christ Himself. The Church is also committed to living in continuity with the patristic Church, and so she looks to the wisdom of the past to sort through the morass of opinions which can easily confuse the present-day discussion. Again, our authors find illuminating facts and patterns that clarify what celibacy really means. Most important: they discover how deeply imbedded this practice is in the history of the Church.

Both scriptural exegesis and historical knowledge would

remain barren, however, were it not for the integrating task of dogmatic theology. Here our authors find that celibacy must be understood against the background of a holistic theology of the priesthood. In fact, the problems with understanding priestly celibacy are often rooted in misunderstandings of the priesthood itself. Many people within the Catholic Church who do not understand celibacy have difficulty because of the practical problems they perceive. Our authors have not neglected the practical questions that arise in the debates over celibacy. They have chosen to show how important it is to have a clergy fully devoted to the Church as the Bride of Christ, by giving the witness of Protestant clergy and their families. Apparently, it is not well known that there are more than a hundred married priests in the Western (Latin) Rite in the United States today, to say nothing of married priests in the Eastern Rites and in other countries, such as England. In the United States, most—if not all—of these married priests have come into the Church after being ordained in other Christian traditions. What is most astounding is that almost all of the married priests are strong advocates of clerical celibacy. They acknowledge that their situations are and should be exceptions to the rule because many of them know from experience the enormous pressures on a man who tries to be both a father to his own children and a spiritual father to the family of God.

This project originated as an inspiration of the Reverend Alphonsus Durran, Father General of the Militant Sons and Daughters of the Immaculate Heart of Mary, better known as Miles Jesu. Through Father Durran's encouragement and generous financial support, I undertook the early stages of organizing this book, drawing on the international scope of the Miles Jesu apostolate. The consecrated lay people and priests of Miles Jesu, especially the Reverend Paul Vota, M.J., made numerous contacts in behalf of this project. Eventually, however, I found myself unable to complete the project, because of the demands of directing a new Catholic institute. In time, I approached the Reverend Peter Stravinskas, who graciously accepted the task of editor as well as contributor. Both Fathers Durran and Stravinskas share the view that there is a great need to defend and promote the discipline of celibacy today. Our hope, and prayer, is that this book will contribute to a more widespread appreciation for, and deep conviction of, the importance of a celibate clergy.

KENNETH J. HOWELL

The Teaching of Christ on Priestly Celibacy

KENNETH J. HOWELL

Priestly celibacy is a much-disputed practice within the Roman Catholic Church today. Many priests and lay people doubt whether the requirement is necessary or valuable, and many more are simply ignorant of the biblical and historical foundations on which the practice is based. All around us we hear calls for the abolition of celibacy. Many in the Catholic Church see the current practice as a lingering but outmoded form of clericalism that would be better set aside. Celibacy, of course, is not limited to the priesthood, since all those who enter religious life are required to make a vow of chastity; but here I limit myself to priestly celibacy. The reader may draw implications for other forms of celibacy.

Presently, I want to argue that the discipline of priestly celibacy is rooted in the biblical teaching on marriage and the Church, and that giving up celibacy would be a momentous and largely hurtful change for the Church. I believe that if people can simply understand celibacy better, they will appreciate more the necessity and benefit of this historically embedded discipline of the Church.

Some important clarifications are important to understand celibacy, since the meaning of the discipline has changed over time. Today, for most people in the West, celibacy means that priests are not allowed to marry. However, we must remember that excluding married men from the priesthood has never been the universal practice of the Church. The Eastern Rite Catholic Churches (e.g., Byzantine) still have a majority of married priests today, and there are a limited number of married priests in the Western or Latin Rite.

Although we do not know how many priests in the early centuries of Christianity were married, we do know some important restrictions applied to them. First, if a man was unmarried at the time of his ordination to the priesthood, he was required to remain unmarried for the rest of his natural life. On the other hand, if a man was married, he was not automatically excluded from consideration. A married man, however, had to accept several conditions upon ordination. He had to vow not to remarry if his wife should die, and he and his wife had to take a vow to refrain from conjugal rights for the sake of the Church. Some assume the reason was so that they would not have any more children and thus incur responsibilities that might understandably limit their service to the Church, but more was involved. Although we do not know for certain when this practice began, a good argument can be made that such vows go back to the time of the original apostles. In those early centuries of Christianity, then, even married priests had a limited form of celibacy—better called continence—because of the nature of the priesthood.

It is further important to distinguish between a doctrine and a discipline. Clerical celibacy is a discipline of Canon Law, not a doctrine of theology. As such, celibacy requirements are much more subject to change than doctrinal matters since changes and exceptions to celibacy are not— *ipso facto*—injurious to the Catholic Faith. Doctrinal beliefs are Tradition that cannot change, while celibacy is a tradition that can. However, it is also important to recognize that the discipline of celibacy is deeply rooted in doctrine and theology. The purpose of this essay is to show just how firmly grounded in the teaching of Christ the discipline of celibacy is.

CELIBACY IN THE TEACHING OF JESUS

The four Gospels have always enjoyed a privileged place in Christian teaching, for they contain our Lord's teachings in their most direct form. Yet only the Gospel of St. Matthew mentions Christ's teaching on celibacy. The importance of this fact will become evident momentarily. Jesus' teaching on celibacy occurs in Matthew 19:10-12:

> The disciples said to him, "If such is the case of a man with his wife, it is expedient not to marry." But he said to them, "Not all men can receive this precept, but only those to whom it is given. For there are eunuchs who have been so from birth, and there are eunuchs who have been made eunuchs by men, and there are eunuchs who have made themselves eunuchs for the sake of the kingdom of heaven. He who is able to receive this, let him receive it."

Jesus' statements on celibacy occur in the context of His reply to the Pharisees' question regarding marriage and divorce (Mt 19:3-6). Jesus reaffirms the teaching of the Old Testament that marriage is permanent and indissoluble. To support this, He quotes Genesis 1:27, "He made them male and female," and Genesis 2:24, "For this reason, a man shall leave his father and mother and be joined to his wife, and the two shall become one." The purpose of creating two sexes, male and female, is to unite man and woman in a permanent bond of matrimony that nothing can dissolve. One of the main purposes of marriage is to reflect the mutual love of the Blessed Trinity in *the* original social institution of the family. It is thoroughly impossible for the members of the Trinity to be broken up or for their mutual love to fail. The Father, the Son, and the Holy Spirit are eternally bound to one another in love. St. Paul also teaches that marriage images the love between Christ and the Church. As Christ's love for the Church is indissoluble, so marriage is indissoluble as well (Eph 5:22-23). Because marriage has this symbolic function of showing God's love among the members of the Trinity and with His people in the Church, it was intended by the Creator to be as permanent in this life as the divine love in eternity.

In the light of Jesus' insistence on the indissolubility of marriage, the Pharisees rightly wondered why Moses allowed divorce (Mt 19:7). Jesus responds that divorce was a temporary provision of the Old Covenant law, which never reflected God's ideal for the family. Jesus says that this temporary allowance was explicitly "because of your hardness of heart" (Mt 19:8, Mk 10:5). But the times now are different. With the coming of the Kingdom of God, Jesus insists that the original bond of marriage is to be fully observed.

When Jesus' disciples understand that divorce is out of the question, they suggest that it is better for a man not to marry (Mt 19:10). They do not give reasons for their objections, but we may assume it was because they saw how difficult the lifelong commitment of marriage would be to maintain. In essence, the disciples say to the Lord, "Maybe it is better to be celibate." Jesus takes the occasion to speak of celibacy for the Kingdom of God. Why would a man want to remain celibate, and not engage in the conjugal rights of marriage? Some have no choice ("from birth"), and others are prevented from marriage by human intervention (Mt 19:12). Presumably, none of Jesus' disciples fell into either of these first two classes. But a third possibility exists. There are still others who freely choose to renounce marriage for the sake of the Kingdom of Heaven.

Jesus' teaching on celibacy occurs in the context of His teaching on marriage, because the usual and expected state for men and women is the loving embrace of marriage in which they find the divine image reflected in marital love (see Eph 5:21-33). Christ's point in Matthew 19:1-9 (and its parallel in Mark 10:1-11) is that marriage is a creation ordinance of God and thus the original pattern God designed for men and women. But by speaking of the Kingdom of God, our Lord was introducing a crucial, new perspective. The Synoptic Gospels (Matthew, Mark, Luke) stress how the Kingdom of God was Jesus' central teaching (cf. Mk 1:15). The Kingdom that Christ inaugurated was the fulfillment of the hope of Israel. His preaching and healing ministry were unmistakable proof of the arrival of the Kingdom (see Mt 11:2-6; Mt 12:24-28). When He speaks of eunuchs "for the sake of the kingdom," He gives the cause or the reason for their celibate state. It differs from the first two celibate states mentioned ("from birth" and "made by men") because the former are involuntary, whereas celibacy for the Kingdom of Heaven is a free choice, a decision made by a free agent.

* * *

Jesus' words about eunuchs for the Kingdom of God raises the question as to what He meant by "eunuchs." The word occurs only in two New Testament contexts, here in Matthew 19:12 and in the story of the Ethiopian eunuch in Acts 8:27ff. In both contexts, the word is used in such a way that the writers assume that the readers will know its meaning without further explanation. This complicates our understanding because the word *eunuch* in English is not a translation, but a transliteration of the Greek *eunouchos*. What does *eunouchos* mean? Oriental and Greek pagan religions used the word to denote men who had castrated themselves in search of union with the deity. Such a concept was completely rejected by the people of Israel, even to the point of excluding from the congregation of Israel those who had emasculated themselves (see Dt 23:1). Furthermore, the castration practiced by some pagan religions went contrary to the divine obligation to "be fruitful and multiply," enjoined in Genesis 1:28. All the Old Testament and Rabbinic Judaism understood marriage and children as a divine obligation. All rabbis, for example, were expected to marry. In the documents of Rabbinic Judaism, we find a distinction between eunuchs who were made so by other men, called *saris-adam* (i.e., Jesus' second group) and those who were incapable of sexual intercourse from birth, called *saris-chamah* (i.e., Jesus' first group). Jesus goes beyond the limits of Rabbinic Judaism by speaking of eunuchs for the Kingdom of Heaven. Given this Old Testament background, Jesus could not have meant eunuchs who undergo physical castration. The first two categories he mentions refer to literal, physical castration, but He could not have intended this in the case of eunuchs for the Kingdom, inasmuch as voluntarily castrating oneself was strictly forbidden in Judaism. Why, then, did Jesus use the word *eunouchos* for someone who dedicates himself to the Kingdom of Heaven? He does so by way of analogy with the first two types of eunuchs, who are not able to marry because of physical limitations. The third category refers to one who, like the first two types, does not marry, but for a different reason: he renounces marriage for the "Kingdom of Heaven." This kind of eunuch was hardly known in Judaism.

"Eunuch" has other connotations in the Old Testament. The Hebrew word for "eunuch", *saris*, indicates a high court official in service to a monarch. Genesis 39:1 speaks of Potiphar as a eunuch of Pharaoh, that is, as one who has judicial authority in Pharaoh's behalf. Second Kings 25:19 likewise speaks of a eunuch as a military official. Most occurrences of *eunuch* are in the Book of Esther, where it indicates a high court official in service to the kings of Persia. And, of course, this royal background is the most natural meaning when St. Luke tells the story of the eunuch from Ethiopia who serves in the court of Queen Candace. There he is called a *eunouchos dunastes* (Acts 8:27), a powerful servant of Candace. In all likelihood, this royal background is the meaning Jesus intended when He spoke of eunuchs for the Kingdom of Heaven. The eunuch for the Kingdom of Heaven is a high court official in Jesus' Kingdom, one who has dedicated himself voluntarily to the exclusive service of the King.

To be a eunuch for the Kingdom of God, then, trumpeted a radical change in the expectation of the culture in which Jesus lived. What will explain this radical call to devote oneself exclusively to the service of the King and His Kingdom? The urgency of embracing the Kingdom in Jesus implied that no other human attachment could take precedence over one's desire to follow the King of the Kingdom. In ancient Judaism, one could not imagine a stronger attachment than marriage and family, reflected in the account of the man who wants to follow Jesus, but who first wishes to return home and bury his father (Lk 9: 59-60). Jusus' words are arresting: "Let the dead bury the dead. Go and proclaim the kingdom of God." Jesus had no intention of denying the importance of marriage and family—His words on the indissolubility of marriage confirm the honor He saw in them—but, compared to the higher calling of His Kingdom, Jesus places first attachment to following Him. Our Lord's words must have sent shock waves through the minds of His Jewish hearers, "And everyone who has left houses, or brother and sisters, or father and mother, or wife and children, for my name's sake, will receive a hundredfold and inherit eternal life" (Mt 19:29; see also Mk 10:28-31 and especially Lk 14:26).

Jesus was aware of how difficult it would be for His disciples and others to accept His teaching on celibacy. If His teaching on the indissolubility of marriage was a stumbling block, His call to celibacy was even more a scandal. This explains why He couched His teaching with warnings. Before laying out the three types of celibates, Jesus emphasized, "Not all men can receive this precept, but only those to whom it is given" (Mt 19:11). Afterward, He reiterates, "He who is able to receive this, let him receive it." It is as if our Lord knew how difficult it would be for many to embrace celibacy for the Kingdom of God. Many in His day, as in ours, could not accept the permanence of marriage; even fewer could accept voluntary celibacy. Nor was everyone called to this vocation, "but only those to whom it is given" (Mt 19:11). He recognized how difficult such a life would be, but He also stressed how important it was for those who advance the Kingdom by taking special places in His work.

I noted above that Jesus' teaching on celibacy occurs only in the Gospel according to St. Matthew. Is there any discernible reason why this should be the case? Why does the parallel passage in Mark 10:2-12 not add the section on celibacy? The answer lies in understanding the distinctive features of Matthew's Gospel, which has rightly been called "The Gospel of the Church." In no other Gospel does

Jesus explicitly use the word *ecclesia*, the normal New Testament word for "church." *Ecclesia* occurs in two important passages in Matthew (16:13-20 and 18:15-20). Although historical-critical interpretation has long maintained that the word *ecclesia* is an insertion by the author of the Gospel, and does not originate from Jesus Himself, no solid historical reason exists to doubt that Jesus Himself intended to establish the Church in these passages. Matthew faithfully transmitted Jesus' teaching on the Church to emphasize the intimate connection between the Kingdom of Heaven and the Church, which, in turn, establishes the meaning and importance of celibacy.

Matthew 16:13-20 recounts the confession of Peter, "You are the Christ, the Son of the Living God." As the confessing apostle, Peter is told that he will be the rock (*petros/petra*) on which Jesus will build His new community, His *ecclesia*. In the flow of Matthew's Gospel, in his telling of the story of Jesus, the word *ecclesia* has not yet occurred. So, what can it mean in this first instance? The main category of Jesus' preaching and healing ministry has so far been the Kingdom of Heaven. When Matthew summed up how Jesus' ministry began, he wrote, "Repent, the kingdom of heaven is at hand" (Mt 4:17). So, a contextual interpretation of Matthew 16:18 requires an answer to the question: How is Jesus' *ecclesia* related to the Kingdom of Heaven? Although we normally translate *ecclesia* as "church" or "community," the word in fact is better translated as "assembly" or "congregation." It was used often in the Septuagint (the Greek translation of the Old Testament) to translate the Hebrew word *qahal*, which was one of the usual terms to denote the people or assembly of Israel. By choosing *ecclesia*, Jesus is saying that the assembly of His disciples will be the ones to carry forth the

Kingdom of Heaven that He brought. In short, Jesus' Kingdom is located in and extended by His *ecclesia*, His Church, founded on Peter as the Rock.

The importance of this text for celibacy lies in the connection between eunuchs and the Kingdom. Matthew 19:12 spoke of those who were "eunuchs for the sake of the kingdom of heaven." Since the Kingdom is manifested primarily in Jesus' *ecclesia* (His Church), those who are Kingdom eunuchs are eunuchs for the Church founded by Jesus. However, Matthew 19:12 does not say explicitly that these eunuchs are for the sake of the Church, but rather "for the sake of the kingdom of heaven." Since the word *ecclesia* was introduced into Matthew's Gospel in chapter sixteen, why would Jesus not use *ecclesia* again if the celibacy being talked about in Matthew 19:12 had anything to do with the Church? The reason has to do with the nature of the Kingdom and the Church. The Kingdom of Heaven is the rule of God brought to earth. As such, it is primarily an invisible and intangible realm that Jesus Himself makes visible and tangible by His presence. Yet the promise of Matthew 16:18 is that Jesus' Church will also continue the invisible rule of God by making it visible and tangible. What Jesus started, the Church continues. So, being a eunuch for the Kingdom of God means being committed to the rule of God, that heavenly reality which is manifested through the Church. Celibacy is not simply a commitment to the Church as an organization, but to the Kingdom of Heaven, which is made known through the Church. A man who takes a vow of celibacy is not doing so because a human organization requires it. He vows a life of celibacy because he is committed to the King and His Kingdom, that is, the heavenly reality made known in the Church as an organization. Jesus calls those who vow celibacy for the

Kingdom "eunuchs" because these people are His high court officials in the Kingdom of Heaven.

IMPLICATIONS FOR THE CATHOLIC CHURCH TODAY

This understanding of celibacy has some very practical consequences. The first is to understand that *we are all called to make God's Kingdom the highest priority of our lives*. Every day we, together with millions of Christians across the globe, pray: "Thy kingdom come. Thy will be done on earth as it is in heaven." Whether we are married or celibate, our call is to be holy, as God's design to build His Kingdom. Building the Kingdom is not primarily something we *do*, but something we *become* by the grace of God. Through sanctifying grace we are transformed, from self-centered people building our own kingdoms, to God-centered builders of Christ's Kingdom. This is another way of saying what is sometimes termed "the universal call to holiness." Part of personal holiness entails placing God's will as the highest priority of our lives. God's will is revealed in Scripture and Tradition, as well as through the teaching of the Magisterium. Our journey through life is a divine opportunity to discover God's will, but each of us does so in different states of life. Every person is called to holiness.

Taking Matthew 19:2-12 as a whole, we find Jesus calling *all of us* to unreserved commitment to the Kingdom of Heaven. For those who marry, their total dedication to the Kingdom requires a lifelong commitment of fidelity. We, like the apostles, can see how demanding such a commitment will be, but living in an indissoluble marriage is Christ's way of building His Kingdom. For a smaller number, Christ calls them to places of special service by voluntarily giving up marriage, so that they can take their rightful places as the court officials of His Kingdom. Celibacy was a radical dedication that was rather new to Jewish culture, but it was necessary because serving the Kingdom of God was to be Jesus' highest priority. Jesus Himself stressed how this state was not for everyone, but only for those "to whom it was given."

In the light of Jesus' teaching, the call to celibacy appears as an exception to the usual rule of marriage and family, in which human beings are nurtured and sustained. Celibacy is not valuable in and of itself apart from the purposes it serves. Unless one knows why he is called to be celibate, the practice is of no value. Celibacy is a call to an unmarried state for the sake of greater attachment to the Kingdom of God. Celibacy makes no sense apart from the marital context of human life that God instituted in the creation of man and woman. Celibacy is a kind of marriage, too, but it is marriage to the whole People of God in the Church, as natural marriage is commitment to one man or woman and the children who are the fruit of marital love.

Just as a married man or woman finds supernatural grace to fulfill one's marital vocation, so men called to priesthood find grace from God to live their calling to be His high court officials for Christ's Kingdom in the Church. Celibacy must be seen primarily as a gift from God, not some arbitrary organizational requirement. The primary question a man must face when he is thinking about priesthood is not celibacy, but whether he is called by God. If God is calling him to priesthood, God will give him the grace to live his celibate calling. Like every other Christian, the priest must depend on God to live his particular calling. Like every other Christian, the priest must depend on God to live out his call to holiness with the special grace God bestows.

If a man sees celibacy merely as an organizational requirement, he is likely to forget why he is called to the celibate life. If, however, he knows that his celibate life is an unreserved commitment to the divine reality of the Kingdom, he will more likely live out his calling in obedience to the organization because he knows that it is God's way of manifesting the realities of the Kingdom. Thus, Jesus' words, "they have become eunuchs for the sake of the kingdom," mean that these eunuchs will be serving Jesus' Church, His *ecclesia*, because the Church makes the invisible Kingdom a visible reality in the world. It also means that their service to the Church is motivated, not by a temporary or passing obedience to a human organization, but to an eternal Kingdom manifested in a divine organism, the Body of Christ.

It is crucial that we not denigrate or despise the call to celibacy. The Church must honor those who have dedicated themselves to the Kingdom by forgoing marriage of their own free will. Priestly celibacy cannot and should not be abandoned because abandoning the practice would be denying our Lord's special call revealed to us in Matthew 19:12. Christ distinctly and clearly taught us that some are called to be "eunuchs for the kingdom of heaven"; and to give up that possibility is to deny some of God's people the opportunity of serving His Kingdom in a celibate life. The Church, from Pope to people, is not free to relinquish any of our Lord's teaching, for the Church is the servant of Revelation, not its master. To abandon His teaching is to abandon Christ Himself. Most will recognize that we are not free to abandon our Lord's teaching on the indissolubility of marriage in Matthew 19:9 and Mark 10:11. We are also not free to abandon His command that some may freely choose the celibate state for the sake of the Kingdom of God.

A look at Church history shows why our Lord opened the possibility of celibacy for some of His "high court officials." Every married couple knows the joyful demands of raising children. In the normal course of life, family responsibilities limit one's ability to serve in extraordinary ways that call one beyond the affairs of married life. The Church has held marriage in such high esteem that she says a married couple must make their highest priority the nurture and education of their children. No married couple may abandon this responsibility under the guise of service to God. Raising children is a married couple's service to God. But married life places temporal and spatial restrictions on a couple that they are not free to relinquish. Being free from family commitments through celibacy allows a man or woman to go to places and forms of service that are not easily accessible to married people. The experience of missions in the Western Rite Catholic Church demonstrates this freedom to a remarkable degree. One reason why the Western (Latin) Rite is by far the largest and most widespread in the world today is that men as celibate priests, and women as celibate Sisters were able to take the Gospel across the globe. This fact in no way denigrates the married priesthood of the Eastern Rites. The Church rightfully celebrates the diversity of liturgies, orders, and local customs in the worldwide Church. There can also be no question, however, that the missionary work of the Church expanded magnificently through the sacrificial lives of priests who were able to leave all for the sake of the Kingdom of God. We as God's People must always honor, encourage, and pray for those who have heard Jesus' special call to be high court officials in His Church.

A Brief History of Clerical Celibacy

REVEREND RAY RYLAND

In the beginning of the Catholic Church, clerical celibacy was optional. Some of the apostles were married men, as were later bishops and priests and deacons. The Eastern Orthodox churches have retained this original tradition of admitting married men to the priesthood. Beginning in the fourth century, the Catholic Church gradually imposed celibacy on her clergy for a variety of reasons. Eventually, in the tenth or eleventh centuries, she made the rule of celibacy binding on all her clergy. . . .

This is the common understanding that non-Catholics and even some Catholics have of the history of priestly celibacy. This understanding is completely wrong. Here are the facts.

The Church's earliest records regarding clerical celibacy are the disciplinary canons of the Council of Elvira (305), in which council all of Spain was represented. These canons deal with infractions of the Church's traditional rules. Because the rules themselves were ancient and presumably well-known, the council gave no explanation. It simply called for obedience. Canon 33 forbids married bishops, priests, and deacons to have sexual relations with their wives and to procreate children. The council reminded the married clergy that they were bound by the obligation of perpetual continence, under penalty of being deposed from the ministry. Though the council does not so specify, we learn from somewhat later sources that both the ordinand

and his wife would have been required to agree to this obligation before he could be ordained. Pope Pius XI, commenting on the Council of Elvira, said these "first written traces" of the "law of ecclesiastical celibacy" "presuppose a still earlier unwritten practice. . . ." [1]

In 314, the emperor Constantine summoned the bishops of the empire to Arles to deal with the Donatist heresy. Like the Council of Elvira, the Arles synod issued various disciplinary decrees, recalling the faithful to authentic teaching. In language quite similar to that of the Elviran canon 33, the council forbade married bishops, priests, and deacons to have conjugal relations with their wives. Infractions of this rule were to be punished by deposition from the ranks of the clergy.

The Council of Nicaea (325) upheld the tradition of priestly celibacy for unmarried and married clergy. In Canon 3 the council proclaimed, "This great synod absolutely forbids a bishop, presbyter, deacon or any of the clergy to keep a woman who has been brought in to live with him, with the exception of course of his mother or sister or aunt, or of any person who is above suspicion." [2] After a careful consideration of fourth- and fifth-century evidence, Cochini concludes that the phrase "any person

---

[1] *Ad catholici sacerdotii*, 43 (1935). An Eastern Orthodox archbishop, Peter L'Huillier, claims that Canon 33, along with other canons, was not promulgated by the Council of Elvira, but was added later. He gives no support for this statement, nor does he say when he thinks the canons were added: *The Church of the Ancient Councils* (Crestwood, N.Y.: St. Vladimir's Seminary Press, 1996), 36. Yet in note 123, p. 89, he admits "it is unquestionable that the canon [33] wants to express a prohibition of marital relations . . . for bishops, priests, and deacons." But see below: the canon must have been added before 314, when the Council of Arles practically quoted it.

[2] Norman P. Tanner, S.J., ed., *Decrees of the Ecumenical Councils*, vol. 1 (Washington, D.C.: Georgetown University Press, 1990), 7.

who is above suspicion" at least includes, if it is not limited to, a wife of a bishop, priest, or deacon who with her husband had taken a vow of continence before he was ordained.[3]

Near the end of the fourth century a Spanish bishop wrote to the pope, asking for help in dealing with a pastoral problem in his diocese. Some of his married clergy were having conjugal relations with their wives and begetting children. In his response in 385, Pope Siricius reminded all the married clergy in Spain [and presumably everywhere else as well] that the law of perpetual continence for married bishops, priests, and deacons is "indissoluble."[4]

The following year, Pope Siricius issued a decretal containing a reminder to all married bishops, priests, and deacons that they were under the law of perpetual continence. He insisted the question was not one of ordering new precepts, but of recalling the clergy to rules long established. Some of the married clergy had tried to defend their continuing conjugal life. Had there ever been a tradition of optional celibacy, the strongest possible argument in their favor would have been to appeal to that tradition.

But the disobedient clergy said nothing about a tradition of optional celibacy. Instead, they appealed to 1 Timothy 3:2 and Titus 1:6 as justifying their conjugal union with their wives. Pope Siricius declared that the phrase "married only once" did not mean that a married bishop could continue conjugal relations after ordination. Instead, "married only once" as an episcopal qualification meant that a man faithful to one wife reasonably could be expected to be sufficiently mature to abide by the perpetual continence

[3] Christian Cochini, S.J., *Apostolic Origins of Priestly Celibacy* (San Francisco: Ignatius Press, 1990), 185-195.
[4] Ibid., 9.

required of him and his wife after he was ordained. This is the first magisterial exegesis of these passages. It is echoed in the writings of the Fathers of this era: Ambrose, Epiphanius of Salamis, Ambrosiaster.[5]

Departing momentarily from our chronological account, we should briefly glance at the *Directory for the Life and Ministry of Priests*, issued in 1994 by the Congregation for the Clergy. Section 59 affirmed the exegesis of the Timothy and Titus passages just given and cited a number of early councils that mandated continence for married, as well as unmarried, clergy. It added that "the Church, *from apostolic times*, has wished to conserve the gift of perpetual continence of the clergy and choose the candidates for Holy Orders from among the celibate faithful (cf. 2 Thess. 2:15; 1 Cor. 7:5; 9:5; 1 Tim. 3:2-12; 5:9; Tit. 1:6-8)" (emphasis added). Married men who with their wives had made a profession of perpetual continence before ordination were, of course, among the "celibate faithful."

Returning to events of the fourth century, we next encounter the Council of Carthage in 390. There the whole African episcopate restated the rule of perpetual continence for all married bishops, priests, and deacons. They insisted they were simply reiterating the unbroken tradition of the Church. The presiding bishop (Genethlius) said about their decree, "*what the apostles taught and what antiquity itself observed*, let us also endeavor to keep" (emphasis added). Some or even many of the African hierarchy, presumably, were married, yet the bishops unanimously declared, "It pleases us all that bishop, priest, and deacon, guardians of purity, abstain from [conjugal intercourse] with their wives

[5] Ibid., note 18, p. 12.

so that those who serve at the altar may keep a perfect chastity."[6]

A decretal, *Dominus inter*, was issued in the early fifth century by a Roman synod led by the pope (probably Pope Innocent I). In reply to questions raised by bishops in Gaul, canon 16 stated, "with regard to bishops, priests, and deacons: those who have the responsibility of the divine sacrifice, and whose hands give the grace of baptism and consecrate the Body of Christ, are ordered by divine Scripture, and not only ourselves, to be very chaste; the Fathers themselves had ordered them to observe bodily continence."[7]

Pontiffs who succeeded Innocent I continued to teach that all clergy, single and married, must strictly observe the traditional clerical continence. We find the same teaching in Jerome, Augustine, and Ambrose. Leo the Great (440-461) stressed this teaching. He also insisted that the wives of bishops, priests, and deacons were to be supported by the Church. The Council of Tours (461) upheld both the ban on married clergy's continuing their conjugal life and the penalty of exclusion from ecclesiastical service for those who disobeyed the ban.[8]

Note a few more instances of this consistent teaching. The Council of Gerona (517) decreed the continuing obligation of perpetual continence for all married clergy, as did the Second Council of Auvergne in 535. Pope Gregory the Great (590-604) reaffirmed this traditional rule. Reflecting the medieval Church's discipline of celibacy, the penitential books of the Celtic churches assert the traditional obliga-

---

[6] Ibid., 5.

[7] Ibid., 15.

[8] Alfons Cardinal Stickler, *The Case for Clerical Celibacy* (San Francisco: Ignatius Press, 1995), 33-41.

tion of perpetual continence for clergy who previously had been married. Married clergy who after ordination continued conjugal relations with their wives were held guilty of adultery and were to be punished accordingly.

The Gregorian reforms of the eleventh and twelfth centuries included dealing with violations of clerical celibacy. The Second Lateran Council (1139) helped carry out this reform. From this fact has grown the false notion that celibacy for bishops, priests, and deacons was *introduced* by this Council. Like all its predecessors that dealt with the issue of clerical celibacy, the Lateran Council was only enforcing the apostolic ban on conjugal life for the clergy.

Tracing this tradition into more modern times, we find the Sacred Congregation for the Propagation of the Faith in 1858 issuing an instruction with this affirmation: "Whoever ponders diligently the true tradition of celibacy and clerical continence will indeed find that, from the first centuries of the Catholic Church, if not by a general and explicit law, at least by behaviour and custom, it was firmly established that not only bishops and priests, but [all] clergy in Holy Orders were to preserve inviolate virginity or perpetual continence."[9]

Yet still some cling to their theory that clerical celibacy was purely optional in the early centuries. They bring forth one bit of evidence for their view. A century or so after the Council of Nicaea in 325, there first appeared in the writings of a fifth-century Eastern historian, Socrates, the story of a man named Paphnutius. According to Socrates' account, the Nicene fathers had considered imposing the

---

[9] Roman Cholij, "Celibacy, Married Clergy, and the Oriental Code," *Eastern Churches Journal*, vol. 3, no. 3 (Autumn 1996), 112.

discipline of perpetual continence on married, as well as on unmarried, clergy. A bishop from Egypt named Paphnutius vigorously opposed the measure and persuaded the Council to allow married clergy to continue their conjugal lives, but still to forbid a man in Holy Orders to marry.

Those who disregard all the evidence thus far laid out and deny the apostolic origin of priestly celibacy draw from the story of Paphnutius two points. They say (1) the story proves that in the early fourth century, married clergy were not under the obligation of perpetual continence; and (2) the Council of Nicaea decided not to impose such an obligation. An Eastern Orthodox advocate of this view calls the Paphnutius episode "the first serious attempt" to "impose [note the verb] celibacy on all the clergy." [10]

There are compelling reasons for rejecting the story of Paphnutius and his alleged intervention at the Council of Nicaea. It has no basis in the tradition. The records of the Council of Nicaea say nothing about it. We have already seen that the Council simply assumed the discipline of perpetual continence for all clergy and sought to safeguard it. The well-known historian Eusebius was present at the Council and wrote about it; he never mentions Paphnutius. Again, consider the events of the times. When the Council of Nicaea was convoked, the Church was locked in a life-and-death struggle with Arianism. The great majority of the Church's bishops were Arian heretics. Why would the council fathers even consider a radical change in the life of the Church which would surely create more human

---

[10] John Meyendorff, *Marriage: An Orthodox Pespective* (Tuckahoe, N.Y.: St. Vladimir's Seminary Press, 1970), 73–74. If Meyendorff is trying to fix the point at which celibacy for all priests, married and unmarried, began to be "imposed," one wonders why he ignores the earlier councils of Elvira (305) and Arles (314).

division within the Church? When the Council of Trullo (discussed below) tried in 692 to justify abolishing the rule of continence for married clergy, the story of Paphnutius could have been its strongest argument. Yet Trullo said nothing about Paphnutius. For a thousand years no Eastern writer advocating clerical marriage mentioned Paphnutius or the alleged decision of the Council of Nicaea not to *impose* perpetual celibacy on married clergy.

Furthermore, the source Socrates names seems extremely unreliable. He says that when he was very young he heard the story from an old man who claimed to have been at the Council of Nicaea. Socrates' alleged informant could have been only a young child when the Council was held. To say the least, it is most unlikely that a child would have been present in council deliberations. So, what is the evidence for the story of Paphnutius' intervention?— Socrates' childhood memory of the childhood memory of an unnamed and unlikely informant.

In a recent book a Greek Orthodox canonist writes that the story of Paphnutius "is probably only a legend fabricated in the East at the beginning of the fifth century." And yet, still clinging to the Eastern claim that celibacy was optional in early centuries, the canonist declares that the fabricated story of Paphnutius "constituted one form of censure in the face of attempts by Rome to impose [note the verb] permanent celibacy on clerics in holy orders." [11] In a definitive study published in 1968, Friedhelm Winkelmann concluded that the episode of Paphnutius has no basis in fact. According to Cochini, Winkelmann's conclusions (with which L'Huillier agrees) are generally accepted among scholars today. [12]

[11] L'Huillier, *Church of the Ancient Councils*, 32.
[12] Cochini, *Apostolic Origins*, 199. See also L'Huillier, note 122, p. 89.

Turn for a moment from historical records to simple reasoning. Those who deny that mandatory celibacy existed from the beginning contend that it originated with the Council of Elvira (305) or at some later date. If this is true, why did the popes and council fathers insist they were not making a new rule, but only upholding ancient tradition? Even more to the point: If celibacy was optional prior to the early fourth century, why would the council fathers and those of later councils impose *on themselves* and on the other married clergy such a drastic and arbitrary discipline? Why did *no one* object that the conciliar rulings were unprecedented?

Or put the issue on a more personal level. Suppose Elvira *did* "impose" a new rule of perpetual continence. Imagine a married bishop going home from the Council. He goes into his house, shouting, "Honey, I'm home!" His wife comes to greet him warmly and then asks, "What were you fellows up to at the council?" The bishop replies, "You could never guess what we decided to do about marriage!" Then he tells her. Incredulous, she shouts, "You decided *what!*" At this point, it would be prudent to stop eavesdropping. But if those who claim celibacy was optional in early centuries were correct, be assured that something like this scene would have been repeated in many clerical homes after the Council of Elvira had taken this drastic action.

In the earlier centuries of the Church, then, the term "priestly celibacy" designated one or the other of two different states of life. It could refer simply to the state of a priest who had never married before ordination. It could refer also to the way of life of married men who, prior to ordination and with the consent of their spouses, had committed themselves to remain continent after ordination.

With this background in mind, consider now the origin of the Eastern Orthodox discipline of optional celibacy (optional for priests, required for bishops). Prior to 692, all the Eastern churches followed the apostolic tradition requiring continence of both married and unmarried clergy. The Council of Trullo in 692 made a radical change in the discipline of celibacy. It issued a number of decrees on the subject. One of the canons confirmed a traditional rule of celibacy: bishops and priests and deacons were forbidden to marry after ordination. Another canon partially affirmed the apostolic tradition: men elevated to the episcopate were forbidden to maintain conjugal relations with their wives after being ordained to the episcopate.

Now comes the change in rules. In canon 13, the Council explicitly (and polemically) set itself against the discipline of Rome; that is, the discipline universally observed up to that time. The council decreed that, henceforth, married men ordained to the diaconate and priesthood could continue in their marital union *after* they were ordained. This decree marked a radical change in the unbroken Eastern and Catholic tradition. In *Ad catholici sacerdotii* (no. 44), Pope Pius XI made an oblique reference to the Eastern departure from the ancient tradition, which he calls "Catholic celibacy." In early times, in the matter of celibacy as in other matters, "there was harmony between the Latin and the Oriental Churches *where accurate discipline flourished*" (emphasis added).

The Trullan Council tried to justify this break with tradition by quoting from the canons of the Council of Carthage (390), whose decrees on celibacy we have already noted. But—and this is very important—the Council changed the wording of the Carthaginian canons to make them agree with Trullo's new rule.

Remember that the Council of Carthage had appealed to apostolic tradition in recalling to perpetual continence all clergy, married and unmarried. According to Trullo, the canon of Carthage mandated only *temporary* continence for the married clergy, and *only* on the days when they were serving at the altar. (This is the Old Testament law for levitical priests serving in the Temple.) Yet despite having radically altered what the Council of Carthage had decreed, the Council of Trullo serenely assured the world that by their new ruling they were only "preserving the ancient rule and apostolic perfection and order. . . ." [13]

The present discipline of celibacy in the Eastern churches (both Orthodox and Catholic) dates from the break made by the Council of Trullo. To an outsider, the discipline raises questions. If a married man can be ordained and live in conjugal union, why cannot a celibate clergyman marry? If a married man can be ordained a deacon and priest and continue in his marital union, why cannot a bishop be married and live with his wife? These apparent inconsistencies are the result of the Eastern churches' having retained only portions of the ancient tradition. The Catholic Church has never allowed a man in Holy Orders to marry because he could not enter conjugal life with his wife. The Church's discipline of celibacy, of course, includes bishops, as well as priests and deacons.

Today some Eastern Orthodox theologians and even an occasional bishop urge further changes in clerical celibacy. They insist that single priests and deacons should be allowed to marry after ordination. They contend further that bishops should be allowed to marry. If adopted, these mea-

[13] Roman Cholij, *Clerical Celibacy in East and West* (Herefordshire, England: Fowler Wright Books, 1988), 115.

sures would completely sever all Eastern Orthodox ties with the apostolic tradition of priestly celibacy.

Given the fact that perpetual continence has always been the Catholic Church's rule for all her clergy, married as well as unmarried, we must ask what is her attitude toward the different discipline of the Eastern churches (both Orthodox and Catholic).

In the past twelve centuries or so, there have been many magisterial references to Eastern Orthodox practice, including some by recent popes. The references have always used guarded language, so as not to widen the breach between the Eastern churches and the Catholic Church. Note the irenic but very clear language used by Pope Pius XI in his 1935 encyclical, *Ad catholici sacerdotii*. Near the end of his discussion of priestly celibacy, the pope stated that nothing he had said about the virtues of priestly celibacy should be construed as blaming or disapproving the different discipline in the Oriental churches. Then he adds: "What We have said has been meant solely to exalt in the Lord something we consider *one of the purest glories of the Catholic priesthood*, something which seems to us to *correspond better* to *the desires* of the Sacred Heart of Jesus *and his purposes* in regard to priestly souls" (no. 47; emphasis added).

In summary: the Catholic Church has acknowledged, tolerated, even spoken with respect for, the Eastern discipline of celibacy only for unmarried clergy and for bishops. But the Church has *never* accepted the Trullan canon (on which the Eastern practice is based) as a valid ecumenical decision. The Church has never said that the Eastern practice is as valid as her own. As we shall see, to do so would contradict what the Church teaches about the charism of virginity and celibacy. Accordingly, the fathers of the Second Vatican Council excluded from *Presbyterorum Ordinis* language that might have suggested that the two differing disciplines are equal in value.[14]

Cholij, himself an Eastern Catholic, characterizes the Catholic Church's attitude toward the Eastern discipline of celibacy in these words:

> ... it is clear that the Oriental discipline of married clergy was always regarded as an exception to general law, towards which Rome showed its indulgence. If this discipline was merely tolerated – and there are good reaons for believing this to have been the case – then the discipline was but a custom of fact, devoid of any legal force."

Furthermore:

> At most, one could perhaps argue that the [Eastern] discipline was legitimate as a concessionary 'privilege' or 'indult.' Even if this were the case, there would still be little ground to argue that Rome thereby implicitly gave its approbation to Canon 13 of Trullo. A privilege of indult permits a practice which is outside of, or contrary to, law. There is no question of abrogation of the law of which the indult is an exception. To approve Trullo on the other hand, would be to abrogate the universal law of continence.[15]

In discussions of clerical celibacy, one often hears conjectures as to whether the next pope will retain or make changes in the present discipline. Is priestly celibacy here to stay in the Catholic Church?

The answer is clearly "yes," and for two main reasons.

[14] Ibid., 190.
[15] Ibid., 187.

The first is that in recent decades the Church has repeatedly emphasized her commitment to this apostolic tradition. Because priestly celibacy *is* an apostolic tradition, the Church has no authority to reject it.

Speaking of clerical celibacy in an address to a Roman synod, January 26, 1960, Pope John XXIII said, "It deeply hurts us that . . . anyone can dream that the Church will deliberately or even suitably renounce what from time immemorial has been, and still remains, one of the purest and noblest glories of her priesthood."

In his 1967 encyclical on priestly celibacy, Pope Paul VI quoted these words of Pope John XXIII (section 37) and spoke of the law of priestly celibacy as "ancient, sacred and providential" (no. 17). He invited all to study the Church's teaching about priesthood and celibacy, so that "the bond between the priesthood and celibacy" will be seen ever more clearly because of "its clear logic" (no. 25). Again, ". . . we consider that the present law of celibacy should today continue to be firmly linked to the ecclesiastical ministry" (no. 14). Vatican Council II had made it possible to ordain mature married men to the diaconate. This provision, Pope Paul declared, "does not signify a relaxation of the existing law, and must not be interpreted as a prelude to its abolition" (no. 8).

Pope John Paul II, in his 1992 apostolic exhortation on priestly formation (*Pastores Dabo Vobis*), repeatedly speaks of clerical celibacy as a *gift*: "a priceless gift," "a precious gift," "a gift of God for the Church." A gift, in other words, to be cherished, not to be ignored or given away. He sees a necessary connection between priesthood and celibacy. The law of priestly celibacy expresses the will of the Church. "But the will of the Church finds its ultimate motivation in *the link between celibacy and sacred ordina-*

tion, which configures the priest to Jesus Christ the head and spouse of the Church." (Does this mean that the law of celibacy is something more than a disciplinary issue?) Then in strong words he adds, "The Church, as the spouse of Jesus Christ, wishes to be loved by the priest in *the total and exclusive manner* in which Jesus Christ her head and spouse loved her" (no. 29; emphasis added).

The Congregation for the Clergy issued its *Directory for the Life and Ministry of Priests* in 1994. Echoing a theme prominent in John Paul II's *Pastores Dabo Vobis*, the *Directory* asserts, "Celibacy is a gift which the Church has received and desires to retain, convinced that it is a good for the Church itself and for the world" (no. 67) Earlier we noted a passage from the *Directory* that declares: "the Church, from apostolic times, has wished to conserve the gift of perpetual continence of the clergy . . ." (no. 59).

Perhaps clearest of all magisterial statements of recent times on the Church's commitment to priestly celibacy is that made by the 1990 Synod of Bishops, Proposition 11. "The synod would like to see celibacy presented and explained in the fullness of its biblical, theological and spiritual richness, as a precious gift given by God to His Church and as a sign of the kingdom which is not of this world—a sign of God's love for this world and of the undivided love of the priest for God and for God's people, with the result that celibacy is seen as a *positive enrichment* of the priesthood." (Does this statement tend to move the issue of priestly celibacy from the realm of discipline to that of doctrine?)

Note, then, this unequivocal language: "The synod does not wish to leave any doubts in the mind of anyone regarding the Church's *firm will* to *maintain* the law that demands perpetual and freely chosen celibacy for present and future candidates for priestly ordination in the Latin rite" (emphasis added).[16]

Therefore, the first reason for saying that priestly celibacy is here to stay is that the Church herself has said so. A second reason is this: The Church's firm commitment to priestly celibacy is expressed perhaps even more strongly in her teaching that the state of consecrated virginity and celibacy is the highest of all human callings. Space permits only a sampling of the Church's statements of this teaching.

In its canons on the sacrament of marriage (session 24), the Council of Trent decreed: "If anyone says the married state is to be preferred to that of virginity or celibacy, and that it is no better or more blessed to persevere in virginity and celibacy than to be joined in marriage, let him be anathema."[17] Pope Pius XII, in his 1954 encyclical *Sacra virginitas*, taught, "The doctrine of the excellence of virginity and of celibacy and of *their superiority over the married state* was ... revealed by our Divine Redeemer and by the Apostle of the Gentiles [referring to 1 Cor 7], so too, it was *solemnly defined as a dogma of divine faith* by the holy council of Trent, and explained in the same way by all the holy Fathers and doctors of the Church. Finally, We and Our Predecessors have often expounded it and earnestly advocated it whenever occasion offered" (no. 22; emphasis added).

Several documents of Vatican II stress the superiority of the charism of virginity and celibacy over that of marriage. *Lumen Gentium*, speaking of the counsels Jesus enjoined on His disciples, says, "Towering among these counsels is that previous gift of divine grace given to some by the

---

[16] Quoted by John Paul II, *Pastores Dabo Vobis*, 29.
[17] Tanner, *Decrees*, vol. 2, 755.

Father... to devote themselves alone *more easily* with *an undivided heart*... in virginity or celibacy" (no. 42; emphasis added). *Optatum Totius* specifies that seminarians should be trained in the duties and dignity of Christian marriage. At the same time, they should "recognize *the greater excellence* of virginity consecrated to Christ, however, so that they may offer themselves to the Lord with fully deliberate and generous choice, and a *complete surrender of body and soul*" (no. 20; emphasis added). *Presbyterorum Ordinis* contains half a dozen similar statements of the superiority of the virginal or celibate state over that of marriage.

The 1967 Synod of Bishops' statement on *The Ministerial Priesthood* contains these words: "While the value of the sign and holiness of Christian marriage is fully recognized, celibacy for the sake of the Kingdom nevertheless *more clearly* displays that spiritual fruitfulness or generative power of the New Law by which the apostle knows that in Christ he is *the father and mother* of his communities." Again, "Through celibacy, priests are more easily able to serve God with *undivided heart* and spend themselves for their sheep, and as a result they are able *more fully* to be promoters of evangelization and of the Church's unity" (emphasis added).[18]

Pope Paul VI, in his 1967 encyclical on priestly celibacy, acknowledged that the married state is a way of sanctity for couples called to matrimony. "But Christ... has also opened a new way [celibacy], in which the human creature adheres wholly and directly to the Lord and is concerned only with Him and His affairs...; thus He manifests in a

---

[18] Austin Flannery, O.P., ed., *Vatican Council II: More Post-Conciliar Documents* (Northport, N.Y.: Costello Publishing Co., 1982), 688.

clearer and more complete way the profoundly transforming reality of the New Testament" (no. 21).

Pope John Paul II expressed the Church's teaching quite simply in 1981 in *Familiaris Consortio*, section 16: " ... the Church, throughout her history, has always defended the superiority of this charism [virginity or celibacy] to that of marriage, by reason of the wholly singular link it has with the Kingdom of God." Five years later he taught, "The 'superiority' of continence to matrimony in the authentic Tradition of the Church never means disparagement of matrimony or belittlement of its essential value." Rather, the "evangelical and authentically Christian superiority of virginity and continence is ... dictated by the motive of the Kingdom of Heaven." [19]

Finally, the 1983 *Code of Canon Law* twice asserts the superiority of the charism of virginity or celibacy. Canon 277.1 describes celibacy as "a special gift of God, by which sacred ministers can adhere more easily to Christ with an undivided heart and can more freely dedicate themselves to the service of God and humankind." Canon 599 speaks in similar terms.

That the charism of virginity and celibacy is the highest state to which a person can be called is Catholic dogma: defined by an ecumenical council, confirmed by the pope, constantly taught by the Magisterium. In the light of this dogma; in the light of the Church's repeatedly emphasizing the intimate link between priesthood and celibacy; in the light of her oft-stated commitment to retaining priestly celibacy, it seems certain that the Church will always cherish and preserve this precious gift God has given her.

---

[19] John Paul II, *The Theology of Marriage and Celibacy* (Boston: Daughters of St. Paul, 1986), 103.

Celibacy and the Meaning of the Priesthood

REVEREND PETER M. J. STRAVINSKAS

More than twenty-five years ago, as a young seminarian, I brought my group of inner-city altar boys to a high school seminary for the day, where they were introduced to priestly formation and the various options that existed within a priestly vocation, including the difference between religious order priests and diocesan or secular clergy. The staff and students were extremely gracious and even allowed the boys the use of the outdoor pool. At the end of the day, the rector informed me that it had been decided the poor kids needed a good meal: thick steaks, french fries, homemade cherry pie, and ice cream. My charges were ecstatic, but one reaction I will never forget. When beholding the culinary delights, fourth-grader Cubit blurted out: "Wooo-ee, if this be poverty, bring on chastity!" Many people, including many practicing Catholics, have no deeper an understanding of clerical celibacy than my ten-year-old server.

I would beg the reader's indulgence to be just a bit autobiographical. I was an only child, went to Catholic schools my whole life, perceived a call to priesthood on the first day of kindergarten (and never wavered from that goal), never met a Protestant until I was in seventh grade, and entered the seminary at the age of seventeen. Now, some will express amazement at such a description of a young life, but, believe it or not, my story could be replicated by thousands of American priests, especially growing up in the Northeast in the nineteen-fifties and -sixties.

Given such a Catholic ethos, certain things were taken for granted—in a good sense. One of them was that a call to priesthood did indeed usually come in one's youth and that it should be acted on as soon as possible, in line with the Lord's remarks about putting one's hand to the plough and not looking back (Lk 9:62). Within that first set of presumptions was another: That if one were to be a priest, he would spend his entire life in the unmarried state. No one ever thought it bizarre or the least bit worthy of discussion—just as normal and natural as the expectation that one's parents would never be divorced.

Then came the late sixties, with the collapse of societal norms, with the questioning of every tradition imaginable, with the misbegotten euphoria of the post-Vatican II era; and attitudes toward priesthood in general and celibacy in particular began to change dramatically. It was in those years that I found myself in the seminary, which is intended by the Church to be an eight-year preparation for priestly life and ministry in every detail. In other words, no newly ordained priest ought ever be able to say truthfully that he was surprised by some essential aspect of his existence, for which he was not given adequate grounding. By 1968, however, thousands of priests had begun a massive exodus from the priesthood; indeed, a departure greater than what the Church experienced at the time of the Protestant Reformation. Sad to report, by the end of the pontificate of Pope Paul VI in 1978, more than a hundred thousand men had petitioned for what is technically known as a "rescript of laicization" and had received one.[1]

---

[1] A rescript of laicization is a document, signed by the Pope, acceding to a man's request to leave the active ministry and to return to the lay state. Under Pope Paul, such a document also usually granted the petitioner a dispensation from celibacy and from the recitation of the

Within that climate, I was supposedly being prepared for ordination. Many of my professors had close friends and classmates who had either left the priesthood or were planning to do so; many of my professors ended up leaving, too. Will anyone be shocked to learn, then, that never once in eight years did I ever (a) have a course in celibacy; (b) have a retreat or day of recollection devoted to the topic; or (c) hear a spiritual conference or homily on that theme? And yet, that is the truth with one notable exception. The few times that the topic of celibacy did come up for discussion, we were told that, by the time we were ordained, celibacy would be optional! More than twenty years into the priesthood, I smile when I think how wishful thinking and ideological conditioning can be so off-base. Engaged couples attending a three-session pre-Cana conference have a better chance of hearing the essentials of married life than my generation of seminarian did in regard to the priesthood. Thanks to the leadership of Pope John

---

Divine Office—two obligations assumed at that time at subdiaconate and now taken on at diaconate. A "laicized" priest remains a priest forever but cannot function as such and, in fact, cannot perform any liturgical role whatsoever, cannot teach theology, and cannot administer any Catholic educational institution.

Not infrequently, we hear people say that we never would have lost all these men if it hadn't been for the law of celibacy. No objective research bears out that assertion. My own personal observation and experience suggest something very different. I knew more than thirty men who had "left the priesthood," only one of whom left precisely to get married. Most left because of disillusionment with the Church or the priesthood in general. Of course, having left and having been dispensed from the promise of celibacy, it would not be odd that they would consider marriage. One final codicil on this aspect of Church history: Statistics show that more than three-fourths of these clerical marriages have ended in divorce, and the Holy See reports that tens of thousands of "laicized" priests have asked to return to active ministry.

Paul II and many good, young bishops, that situation has changed for the better.

Having had many wonderful priest-friends throughout childhood and adolescence, and having lived celibacy for twenty-five years before ordination, I think I did understand both the expectations of the Church and the practical pitfalls. Very early in my priestly life, I became involved in ecumenical work. The one, consistent theme I heard from non-Catholic clergy was how wise the Catholic Church was to mandate celibacy for her clergy. Why? These ministers told me three things: (1) Optional celibacy means mandatory marriage; that is, any man who would freely choose celibacy would be thought to have a questionable sexual orientation, in the minds of most congregations. (2) Marriage and ministry do not go together, so little that most of their wives were miserable and most of their children had an unabated resentment toward organized religion because of their perception of having been cheated out of a father by "the Church." (3) Having a married minister does not eliminate sexual scandals; truth be told, Protestant clergy have an even higher share of such, with adultery, pedophilia, and homosexual liaisons occurring with depressing regularity.[2] I took seriously the counsel of these brothers in Christ and have never forgotten it.

---

[2] John Henry Cardinal Newman saw this very clearly when he wrote—over a century ago—from his stance as a former Anglican clergyman: "... I state my deliberate conviction that there are, to say the least, as many offenses against the marriage vow among Protestant ministers , as there are against the vow of celibacy among Catholic priests. ... But if Matrimony does not prevent cases of immorality among Protestant ministers, it is not celibacy which causes them among Catholic priests. It is not what the Catholic Church imposes, but what human nature prompts, which leads any portion of her ecclesiastics into sin. Human nature will break out, like some wild and raging element,

A THEOLOGY OF CELIBACY

While all of the above information may be interesting, it still does not explain why the Catholic Church requires celibacy of her priests who belong to the Latin Rite.[3] Of course, and in truth, the connection between priesthood and celibacy is not unique to Catholicism. We find such linkage in various pagan cults of Greece and Rome and, even more radically, in Stoicism's overall rejection of sexual pleasure. While these historical precedents may offer interesting angles of insight or a "natural" intuition in this regard, Christian faith sees something much deeper here.

Catholics believe that through the Sacrament of Holy Order, a man is "configured" to Christ the High Priest. In other words, no Catholic priest "has" a priesthood of his own; rather, he shares in the priesthood of the one and only Priest of the New Covenant, Jesus Christ. Our participation in that priesthood needs to be as full and visible as possible; "maleness" is one such sign, and celibacy is another. The first is an absolute, while the second is not—

---

under any system; it bursts out under the Protestant system; it bursts out under the Catholic; passion will carry away the married clergyman as well as the unmarried priest. . . . Till, then, you can prove that celibacy causes what Matrimony certainly does not prevent, you do nothing at all" (*Lectures on the Present Position of Catholics in England*).

[3] It should be noted that the Catholic Church consists of many "rites," which differ in some accidentals (such as liturgical forms and discipline), all the while professing one faith, in communion with the Bishop of Rome. The Latin or Roman Rite is the largest by far of them all and is actually larger than all the others put together; this rite and a few other so-called "Eastern" or "Oriental" rites mandate celibacy, while the others permit a married man to be ordained, albeit he cannot remarry should his wife die, and bishops are chosen solely from the ranks of the celibate clergy.

although the appropriateness of the sign of celibacy touches very closely on the nature of the priesthood.

Jesus was a priest at the core of His being, which is to say that He did not simply function as a priest on certain occasions (e.g., in offering Himself to the Father on Good Friday); rather, His entire life was an oblation given to the Father, thus uniting within Himself the roles of Victim and Priest. The priests of the Old Covenant functioned at the Temple according to a schedule; while "on duty," they lived at the Temple to ensure ritual purity. Among other things, that meant abstaining from marital intercourse. The tenth chapter of the Epistle to the Hebrews teaches us that our great High Priest fulfilled all those holy sacrifices by His one eternal offering; in that moment, He also abolished priestly functionalism. That is, priesthood is not what one *does* but who one *is*. Since the Lord's entire life was a priestly offering, His observance of continence was not an on-again, off-again phenomenon. And it was the self-same approach to which He called His disciples when He urged them to leave house, wife, brothers, parents, and children "for the sake of the kingdom of God" (Lk 18:29).

Therefore, we see that the Twelve, although probably many of them were married, were obedient to the Master's command; they left all to follow Him in a radical response to prepare the way for that time and place in which "men neither marry nor are given in marriage" (Mt 22:30). Was this expected? Hardly. Judaism had a keen sense of the meaning and beauty of marriage and family.[4] Jesus'

[4] Yet, even within Judaism, one finds certain of the prophets living celibately, and convincing evidence from Qumran suggests that at least some members of that community lived in celibacy. Interestingly enough, rabbinic literature also recounts a tradition that Moses—after beholding God on Mount Sinai—never again had sexual relations with

approach went against the goad here, but that was not the only instance of such a departure from the expected pattern of teaching or behavior on His part. Can we forget that for centuries Jewish law had permitted divorce and remarriage? Our Lord's reversal of that norm was so unexpected that it caused the disciples to suggest that perhaps it might be better not to marry at all (Mt 19:10)! The Savior was not simply pleased to be counter-cultural (although He was certainly that); He was quite intent on presenting Himself—and any who wanted to be a part of Him—as eschatological signs, that is, as living pointers to the age to come, wherein every human good (even married love) is subsumed into the *Summum Bonum* (the Highest Good), allowing God to be "all in all" (1 Cor 15:28).

Clear evidence from the Early Church, discussed elsewhere in this volume,[5] demonstrates that when married men were admitted to the priesthood, they and their wives gave up their marital rights and lived as brother and sister.[6] With the passage of time, the Church in the West took a

---

his wife, the obvious implication being that once one had seen God, all other relationships and loves paled into insignificance. See, in this regard, Anthony Opisso's "The Perpetual Virginity of Mary in the Light of Jewish Law and Tradition," in *The Catholic Answer* (July-August 1996).

[5] Roman Cholij, *Clerical Celibacy in East and West* (Herefordshire, England: Flower Wright Books, 1989); also Christian Cochini, *Apostolic Origins of Priestly Celibacy* (San Francisco: Ignatius Press, 1990).

[6] Indeed, St. Paul speaks of various apostolic men who are accompanied, not by a "wife" (as some mischievous English translations put it), but by a "sister" (1 Cor 9:5), that is, a Christian woman who tended to the needs of these men in much the same way as the women who accompanied Jesus (Lk 8:1-3).

The movement away from married clerics who abstained from sexual intercourse when "on duty" toward demanding "perfect continence" is already documented in the *acta* of the Council of Carthage in 390. Furthermore, the reason given for this discipline is the intercessory and

slightly different tack by calling only men who showed a capacity to live the charism of celibacy, not unlike the Lord's admonition found in Mt 19:12.

The first major departure from the expectation of priestly continence occurred with the Council of Trullo.[7] Its most problematic canon dealt with clerical marriages and effectively turned the entire Tradition on its head by not only permitting married men to be ordained but by allowing for their continued use of marital rights. The legislation, however, was rather convoluted and demanded continence before a priest could celebrate the Eucharist. In many ways, unwittingly, Trullo set the stage for what later became the Protestant notion of priesthood, reducing priesthood to a liturgical role. The ontology of Holy Order (namely, that a man is changed in his very being, which identity is a constant aspect of his existence) had been downgraded to functionalism (namely, that a man is a priest when he is "doing" something priestly). *Doing* had replaced *being*—the very dichotomy the eternal High Priest had reversed. Not surprisingly, ten centuries later, the functional concept of priesthood among the Protestant

---

mediatory nature of the priesthood *in se* and not merely through isolated mediatory or liturgical acts. Another point to note regarding Carthage's dealing with the matter is that bishops, priests, and deacons alike fall "under the same obligation of chastity" because of their liturgical ministry, indeed, their liturgical way of life. Finally, it is worth observing that already in 390 we find an emphasis on the fact that the fathers of Carthage are not inventing new legislation but simply enforcing what was "taught by the apostles and observed *by antiquity itself*" (Cochini, 4-5; emphasis added).

[7] This council was an Eastern regional synod, convoked ten years after the Second and Third Councils of Constantinople and intended to enact disciplinary canons. This controversial synod had to wait nearly two centuries to find a Roman Pontiff to ratify its laws—and then only cautiously.

Reformers came to allow, and even demand, the departure of mandatory celibacy.

Besides the ontological nature of the priesthood, celibacy is particularly appropriate because Catholic theology assigns a sacramental meaning to Matrimony as well as to priesthood. It was undoubtedly this very notion which brought Paul to conclude that the married state and full-time discipleship were in conflict (see 1 Cor 7:32–33). Now, while some observers have argued that Paul simply had a negative assessment of marriage, an objective reading of the passage will not bear out such a reading. It would seem that Paul is saying, however, that given the radical nature of Christian discipleship and the pressing (and good) demands of marriage, the two states are incompatible within one person. Seen in this light, what the Apostle was holding out for and what the Latin Church has opted for is an understanding of Matrimony and Holy Order as both deserving of a full commitment, with no divided existence. Far from being a negative judgment on marriage, then, the Church's position exalts Christian marriage and urges taking that vocation and sacrament seriously—as seriously as priestly ordination.

Clerical celibacy also bears an eschatological meaning, that is, it points man here below to a life to come. As we saw earlier, our Lord Himself spoke about this dimension when He reminded His audience that in the age to come human beings take on an angelic aspect as they exchange their physical desires for contemplation (see Mt 22:30). Celibacy, then, is not simply a lifestyle, it is a message—a prophetic message—that helps the human race in general and Christians in particular to remember that there is more to life than the sensual and encourages them not to get lost in the ephemeral. In our contemporary, sex-saturated world, this word needs to be spoken as often and as loudly and clearly as possible. In fact, the silent presence of Catholic clergy and religious on the streets of the secular city constitutes a most eloquent testimony to the existence of the transcendent and stands as an on-going invitation to the world to move beyond that which is passing; this witness is not unlike that of Ezekiel, who is told by the Lord that his very life should stand as a sign for the people (Ezek 24:24). The priest, as an *alter Christus*, experiences in his person a foretaste of the life of heaven by being focused solely on God; and, on the basis of his personal experience, he likewise appeals to his fellow men to follow him as He has followed Christ. The Eucharistic Sacrifice, the eschatological sign *par excellence*, is similarly celebrated most fittingly by one who is himself an eschatological sign. In 1988, then-Archbishop J. Francis Stafford summed up this aspect of clerical celibacy thus:

> Since Christ was unmarried, we may find it strange at first that the [Second Vatican] Council speaks of fatherhood in Christ. Yet the hymn *Summi Parentis Filio* speaks of Christ as father of the world to come. If we bear in mind what St. Paul teaches us about the spousal love of Christ for His Church, we will see that this "world to come" is nothing less than the child of that union, the fruit of that love.... It is not for nothing that the priest is addressed as "Father" by his people.
>
> As with the fatherhood in Christ, that of the priest points to the world to come: His solitude and earthly barrenness, a prefiguring of death; his prayer, pastoral charity and spiritual fruitfulness, a sign of God's power which is at work now to sanctify and so to yield eternal life.[8]

[8] J. Francis Stafford, "The Mystery of the Priestly Vocation," *Origins* 18.22 (Nov. 10, 1988).

CELIBACY IN PRACTICE

While the Church has always taught that the celibate form of life, chosen for the Kingdom, is higher than other forms of life, she has also taught that the celibate person is not thereby automatically granted access to holiness of life. States of life are conceptual and objective; persons are actual and subjective. Therefore, it is important to note that, objectively speaking, a consecrated celibate *ought* to be holier than anyone else in the Church, but we also know that that does not necessarily happen in all cases. The theology of celibacy—like the theology of marriage—can be diminished or even perverted when lived by weak, sinful human beings. And so, it might be well to round out our reflections by looking at what the charism of celibacy can and should do for both the individual and the Church, as well as offering some practical observations about its living.

Several "negatives" might be grouped together to advantage:

(a) Celibacy is not merely a "rule" or "external norm." Or, as Pope John Paul II warned in a post-synod apostolic exhortation on priestly formation: "For an adequate priestly spiritual life, celibacy ought not to be considered and lived as an isolated or purely negative element, but as one aspect of a positive, specific and characteristic approach to being a priest" (*Pastores Dabo Vobis*, no. 29). When viewed from a juridical or legal perspective, this style of life can appear almost inhuman and is certainly robbed of its inner meaning and beauty, just as marriage would be if deemed little more than a "remedy for concupiscence." Rather, celibacy is a charism freely bestowed by the Lord upon certain members of His Church, for the salvation of those individuals and for the good of the whole Church and the salvation of the entire world. Just as it is freely bestowed, so too must it be freely received, never simply grudgingly endured but always joyfully and lovingly embraced. When celibacy is seen as a burden, neuroses surface, as does aberrant behavior, made manifest in repression or unhealthy forms of compensation. Which leads to the next point.

(b) Celibacy is not bachelorhood. When regarded as merely being unmarried, celibacy devolves into a lifestyle in which material comforts, the drive for power, or ambition replaces sexual pleasure. Not a few priests have been heard to say, "My Cadillac is my wife!"—a theologically and spiritually precarious, as well as a psychologically devastating, attitude.

(c) Celibacy is not contrary to human nature. Interestingly, *The New Celibacy*, by Gabrielle Brown, a nonbeliever, offers some of the strongest support for this way of life. Her research is professional and dispassionate, and therefore well worth reading.[9] Father Stanley Jaki's study also contains fascinating endorsements of celibacy (or at

[9] In that volume, we find statements like the following:

"There are many priests, nuns and monks who have confronted and accepted their sexual natures so completely that they are happily and comfortably celibate."

"Freud was surprisingly open to the positive results of celibacy. He observed that people can achieve happiness by transcending sexuality for a higher experience of love and took examples from religious life."

"Celibacy can both strengthen a man and soften him."

"In ancient Rome, despite its dissolute reputation, the effort of continence was greatly admired and thought to represent a superior nature and a character verging on the divine."

"Love is less likely to be restricted in its nonsexual expression than in a love relationship focused on that one overriding concern—which often occurs when sexuality dominates the relationship."

"Those (celibates) who have achieved a permanent state of pleasure

least back-handed compliments) from such unlikely sources as Ignaz Döllinger, George Sand, Friederich Nietzsche, Rolf Hochhuth, George Bernard Shaw, and Ernest Renan.[10]

(d) Choosing celibacy is not a matter of opting for what is good (celibacy) over what is bad (marriage), but of considering two "goods" and selecting one that is objectively better. As was noted earlier, pitting one style of life against another is counterproductive and unbiblical. Celibacy is not a statement against anything; it is a statement in favor of something—the Kingdom of God and eternal life. Pastoral experience demonstrates that when married life is highly valued, celibate vocations flower in the Church; similarly, priestly celibacy gives powerful support to married couples. Consecrated celibacy and Christian marriage are not in competition or rivalry with each other; they complement each other, as marriage is a sign of Christ's present love for His Church and celibacy points to the future consummation of that love in heaven.

One of the consistent objections leveled against clerical celibacy is that the temptations of modern society are "too great" to sustain such a burden. Let's examine that statement a bit. Following such logic, one would have to conclude that, given the promiscuous nature of most sexual activity today, commitment to a spouse in a stable, permanent, and exclusive union is equally untenable. We know, however, that the Latin proverb has it right in asserting, *Abusus non tollit usum* (Abuse doesn't take away use). In

---

or fulfillment are said to radiate a kind of energy of love which is constant, unbounded, brilliant, and truly universal."

"Celibacy is a style of life known only to humans."

[10] Stanley Jaki, *Theology of Priestly Celibacy* (San Francisco: Ignatius Press, 1998).

other words, the mere existence of the possibility of a problem does not automatically rule out the correct use of a particular faculty or institution. Rather, the solution is to return to the sources for a kind of refresher-course at both the intellectual and affective levels. Temptations against marital fidelity are not inventions of the twenty-first century; they are as old as the institution of marriage. Love, commitment, prayer, and hard work are the keys needed to ensure fidelity. The same keys are needed to maintain a celibate commitment. If a priest took seriously the centrality of Holy Mass and the Divine Office in his daily life and worked hard in his pastoral endeavors, he would generally be well insulated from the most egregious assaults on his consecrated celibacy. Furthermore, when priestly identity is strong and one's priestly life is fulfilling, celibacy is rarely if ever a difficulty—not unlike observing marital chastity for the happily married.

Of course, one cannot gainsay the importance of personal discipline in all this. Fifteen centuries ago, St. Augustine (who had ample personal experience with sexual licentiousness) asked this telling question: "Why do you follow your own flesh? Turn round, and let your flesh follow you" (*Confessions*, bk. 4.11). In other words, emotions must be ruled by the intellect—whether those emotions are grounded in ordinary physical or biological urges or in a desire for companionship and human love. It is extremely important for future priests to be taught how to be alone without being lonely. Many married people can testify—sadly—that although they have shared a house with a spouse for decades, they lead lonely and disconnected lives. Priestly solitude should be a most welcome aspect of a life that seeks to develop the mind and a contemplative mode of existence. Developing interesting and healthy hobbies is also critical for appreciating one's own company, while keeping loneliness at bay. Good priestly fraternity is the best way to guarantee that one is not over-powered by lonesomeness. Employing these safeguards to clerical celibacy is no more than what the Second Vatican Council referred to as "mak[ing] use of all the supernatural and natural helps which are now available to all" (*Pres-byterorum Ordinis*, no. 16). As Pope John Paul II has said, "it is prayer, together with the Church's Sacraments and ascetical practice, which will provide hope in difficulties, forgiveness in failings, and confidence and courage in re-suming the journey" (*Pastores Dabo Vobis*, no. 29).

Sometimes we hear it said that married priests would be better counselors and role models to their flocks, in that 95 percent of the lay faithful are married. Once more, the assertion does not hold up under scrutiny. Must an oncologist have cancer in order to deal effectively with cancer? Must a teacher revert to childhood to "relate" her-self to first-graders? Nor can one point to an iota of evi-dence that married Protestant clergy and rabbis have any greater effectiveness in pastoral situations with the married than do celibate priests. In fact, the only serious research on the topic, conducted by the priest-sociologist Andrew Greeley, showed clearly that young married women actu-ally prefer celibate priests as their spiritual "confidants" for a variety of reasons, not the least of which is that such relationships seem to enhance their relationships with their husbands.[11]

Not infrequently yet another challenge to celibacy is

---

[11] Aidan Nichols, "Celibacy as Witness," *The Tablet* (Aug. 26, 1989), 968-970. This same article also mentions *en passant* that "the burden of being a married priest is pretty heavy too, *especially for the priest's wife*" (emphasis added).

raised with the claim that, while celibacy may have "worked" in another time and place, it can't do so today in a host of locations from North America to Africa to Latin America. The argument usually continues on to say that this is no more than giving due consideration to inculturation and acknowledging the "coming of age" of regional Christian communities. But if—as we have attempted to show—celibacy *is* related to the ontological nature of the priesthood and *is* intimately tied to the eschatological dimension of Christian life and *was* clearly an integral part of Christ's invitation to apostleship, how can we treat it as an expendable commodity? Father Aidan Nichols handles this challenge to celibacy most deftly when he writes: "To say that local churches, in given parts of the globe, cannot be expected to produce celibate ministers of the Gospel is to say that they cannot be expected to reproduce an intrinsic element in the experience of the apostles. And this seems a strange way in which to recognize the Christian maturity of such churches!" [12]

In other words, this approach is—in reality—a slap against a particular culture, essentially holding that the evangelical commitment or sexual self-control of its time or place is so minimal that potential priests in its environment are incapable of doing what priests have done for centuries. To debate the topic incessantly is actually to do a great disservice to potential candidates, especially when one reads of the determination of the 1990 synod in this regard: "The Synod does not wish to leave any doubts in the mind of anyone regarding the Church's firm will to maintain the law that demands perpetual and freely chosen celibacy for

[12] Aidan Nichols, *Holy Order: Apostolic Priesthood from the New Testament to the Second Vatican Council* (Birmingham, England: Veritas, 1990), 164.

present and future candidates for priestly ordination in the Latin Rite." [13]

The contention is occasionally made that insistence on a celibate clergy is ecumenically counter-productive. No less a priest-scholar and ecumenist than Father Raymond Brown takes on this objection forthrightly: "Precisely because the witness of celibacy is conspicuously lacking in many other Christian churches, the Roman Catholic Church has an ecumenical *duty* to the Gospel to continue to bear an effective witness on this score" (emphasis added). He goes on:

> Perhaps this would be possible without a law, but one must admit that it is the law of priestly celibacy that makes it clear that those who accept it ar doing so for the sake of Christ and not simply because they prefer to be bachelors. Some of the forms of optional celibacy being proposed would soon lead to obscuring the vocational character of celibacy and would reduce it to a personal idiosyncrasy.[14]

We often tend to forget that ecumenism is a two-way street. While Catholics surely have many things to learn from their separated brethren, our non-Catholic brothers and sisters also have a few things to learn from Catholics—and the value of a celibate clergy is one of those things, in my estimation.

The most obvious benefit of celibacy is pastoral, as it "is lived in an atmosphere of constant readiness to allow oneself to be taken up, as it were 'consumed,' by the needs and demands of the flock" (*Pastores Dabo Vobis*, no. 28). In

---

[13] Cited in *Pastores Dabo Vobis*, no. 29.

[14] Raymond E. Brown, *Priest and Bishop: Biblical Reflections* (London: Chapman, 1970), 26.

saying this, Pope John Paul II was merely echoing the fathers of the Second Vatican Council, who declared that "this perfect continence for love of the Kingdom of Heaven has always been held in high esteem by the Church as a sign and stimulus of love, and as a singular source of spiritual fertility in the world" (*Lumen Gentium*, no. 42). Who can fail to be impressed by the missionary labors of millions of priests in history or the witness of thousands more in the gulags and concentration camps of this century? Can one doubt that their celibacy allowed them—even challenged them—to be such constant and faithful signs of Christ's saving message of truth and love? Humanly speaking, could we have expected such dramatic testimony from one rightly concerned for the welfare of a wife and children? Much less dramatic—but no less impressive—is the pastoral service of hundreds of thousands of celibate priests whose day begins before sunrise and ends as the clock's hands move into a new day. Like a candle, the celibate priest fulfills his mission by "burning himself out" for Christ, His gospel, and His Church.

Apart from these more "pragmatic" considerations on celibacy,[15] a quick re-reading of what I have written here shows that I have often relied on comparisons between priesthood and marriage. And I think that, although accidental in part, this tendency has been fortuitous. Both vocations are highly demanding, requiring tremendous amounts of self-sacrifice. In fact, I am reminded of an exhortation that once formed part of the Sacrament of Matrimony. The bride and groom were instructed that for a

[15] Two other "practical" works on the subject are: Peter M. J. Stravinskas, *Essential Elements of Religious Life Today* (Libertyville, Ill.: Marytown Press, 1987), and Federico Suarez, *About Being a Priest* (Princeton, N.J.: Scepter Publishers, 1996).

marriage to succeed, self-sacrifice had to become a fixture in the relationship. But the text went on to note, both realistically and hopefully: "Sacrifice is usually difficult and irksome; love can make it easy; perfect love can make it a joy." It is the Church's conviction—after centuries of experience—that perfect love can make celibacy a joy for the priest himself and for the whole Church he serves.

Pulling together theology and spirituality, we bring to mind that as all was being consummated on Calvary, we encounter three virgins—Jesus, Mary, and John—forming the *ecclesiola*, the "little Church" about to be born from the wounded side of the Lord. That Church embodied the seeds of a virginity destined to bear fruit, both in time and unto eternity. It is the Church's hope and desire that her celibate clergy (and her consecrated religious too) would show forth to the world, in a unique manner, the Church's identity as both the virginal mother and the fruitful spouse of Christ.

Proposition 11 of the 1990 synod on priestly formation embodied this hope:

> The Synod would like to see celibacy presented and explained in the fullness of its biblical, theological and spiritual richness, as a precious gift given by God to His Church and as a sign of the Kingdom which is not of this world, a sign of God's love for this world and of the undivided love of the priest for God and for God's People, with the result that celibacy is seen as a positive enrichment of the priesthood.[16]

This book is itself a small effort toward the realization of that desire of the synod fathers.

[16] Cited in *Pastores Dabo Vobis*, no. 29.

Marriage and the Priesthood

JOHN M. HAAS

There are few Catholic men with wife and family who have had to face the choice of becoming a priest or remaining a layman. I am one of the few. Late in my thirties and with a number of children, I had to decide whether I could fulfill my vocation as a Catholic more effectively in the clerical or lay state. In other words, I had to choose to be a layman.

Few in the Church are ever presented with the necessity of choosing the lay state. Some, after great prayer and reflection, may choose *not* to become priests. Usually, however, this is a decision that God has *not* called them to the priesthood, rather than a positive choice on their part. The vast majority of men in the Catholic Church, having never struggled with the possibility of a vocation to the priesthood, simply spend their lives as laymen without engaging in a specific choice to *be* laymen. They have always been in the lay state and they simply continue in it.

The decisions most laymen struggle with have to do with more mundane matters. What should be my major course of study in college? To which graduate schools should I apply? Do I really want her to be my wife? I've been out of work for three months now; I wonder if I should try the job market in Dallas? All of these decisions are of tremendous importance in the life of a man, and each provides an opportunity for growth in God's grace. But usually a man does not consciously choose that condition within which all those worldly decisions take place—that of being a layman.

The "pastoral provision"

In 1982, the Holy See issued a directive known as the "Pastoral Provision," granting permission for certain married clergymen of the Episcopal Church in the United States to be ordained priests in the Catholic Church and to continue in their normal family relationships. Since I had been an Episcopal clergyman before becoming Catholic, I found myself faced with the task of deciding whether I should be a layman or a priest. It was not an easy decision, since I had enjoyed the ministry tremendously, but after much prayer and reflection I decided that God had called me to be a layman. In other words, I *chose* the lay state.

I knew full well that there were occasions when the Holy See permitted the ordination of married men to the priesthood. It was allowed out of esteem for the venerable traditions of the Eastern Churches and out of pastoral considerations for Protestant clergymen who later came to the Faith. But through my reflections I came to see why this was historically the exception rather than the norm. This period of discernment led me to consider the Catholic vocation to family life and to the priesthood in light of one another and to consider what each vocation demanded of a man. I came to the conclusion that it would be nearly impossible to live both vocations at once.

Centrality of sacrifice

During my conversion process, one of the things I had found to be most striking about the Catholic Church was the centrality of the notion of sacrifice. In the center of Catholic churches stood the crucifix, the representation of Christ's sacrificial death, which brought about the redemption of the world. The principal act of worship was the Sacrifice of the Mass, by means of which the Church offered the reconciling oblation of Christ to the Father. The culmination of that liturgy was the People of God actually eating the sacrificial Victim. Entrance into the Catholic Church was brought about by entering into Christ's own sacrifice, by dying and rising with Him in the waters of Baptism. And the ministry of the clergy in the Catholic Church was a sacrificial one. As expressed in the Second Vatican Council's decree on the life and ministry of priests: "Through the ministry of priests the spiritual sacrifice of the faithful is completed in union with the sacrifice of Christ the only mediator, which in the Eucharist is offered through the priests' hands in the name of the whole Church in an unbloody and sacramental manner until the Lord Himself come. The ministry of priests is directed to this and finds its consummation in it" (*Presbyterorum Ordinis*, no. 2).

Priests also personally sacrificed the opportunity of having a family in order to serve the Church in fuller imitation of Christ. And as I reflected on it, I saw that for Catholics a vocation to marriage was also a sacrificial one, entailing a surrender of the spouses to one another and, together, to their children. So it seemed that sacrifice was at the heart of every Catholic reality. More than that—it seemed that the Church was able to see the cross (i.e., sacrifice) standing at the heart of reality itself.

It seemed to me that the principal characteristic of Catholic life and piety was personal sacrifice joined to our Lord's own oblation on Calvary. No matter one's state in Christian life, it was to be characterized by sacrifice. When this fact is considered in terms of the lay or the priestly state, it is easily recognized that the types of sacrifices called forth will be different—distinct and practically mutually exclusive. If a man lived his married vocation to its sacrificial fullness, it would be almost impossible for him to live the priesthood with the same sacrificial abandon. A total surrender to one way of life almost precludes the other, even though we know that celibacy "is not demanded of the priesthood by its nature" (no. 16). The Church has, admittedly, permitted married priests over the centuries but invariably as an exception and a concession.

Marriage is thus seen as an obstacle to the fullness of the priestly life and to the witness it can offer the world. Conversely, one can say that the priesthood likewise can constitute an obstacle to a full living out of the vocation of husband and father and to the witness it provides the world.

THE PRIEST'S SACRIFICE

The priest's life is linked inextricably, indeed mystically, to our Lord's sacrifice. Jesus came as the sacrificial Victim to be offered as a ransom for many. As such, He was a perfect oblation, offered in its entirety, without any equivocation, without any reservation, without spot or blemish, to the Father. The priest, by God's grace and the efficacy of the sacrament, joins himself to that sacrificial Victim. He foregoes, as did our Lord, family and wealth and worldly ambition, so that there will be no equivocation, no compromise, in his total surrender to the Father in union with the Paschal Lamb.

It is this very abandonment and total surrender of all he has and is which bears the greatest fruit. Through it, he raises up other priest-victims, not according to the flesh, but according to the spirit. "The Shepherd and Bishop of our souls set up His Church in such a way that the people whom He chose and acquired by His blood should always until the end of the world have its own priests, for fear Christians would ever be like sheep that have no shepherd" (*Presbyterorum Ordinis*, no. 11). So the celibacy and renunciation of family life by priests are not conditions of sterility, but the source of tremendous fertility.

The fruitfulness of priests is seen not only in raising up sons to follow them in their vocation, but preeminently in their applying to the world the redemptive fruits of Christ's sacrifice through their very lives. "They are consecrated to God in a new way in their ordination and are made the living instruments of Christ the eternal Priest, and so are enabled to accomplish throughout all time that wonderful work of His which, with supernatural efficacy, restored the whole human race" (no. 12). Priests themselves, in their very lives in union with Christ, effect His salvation in the world. This is why their lives center on the offering of the Mass. "In the mystery of the Eucharistic Sacrifice, in which priests fulfill their principal function, the work of our redemption is continually carried out. . . . So when priests unite themselves with the act of Christ the Priest they daily offer themselves completely to God . . . " (no. 13).

It is this moral, personal, and sacramental act of complete self-sacrifice which most characterizes the life of the priest. "This sacrifice is therefore the center and root of the whole life of the priest, so that the priestly soul strives to make its own what is enacted on the altar of sacrifice" (no. 14).

If his is a life of complete surrender in Christ to the Father in service to the world, how can the priest compromise it with wife and children? By his uniting himself with Christ, the world itself has become his family and everyone in it has a claim on him, as they do on Christ Himself.

We all know that such a life of complete abandonment is difficult. The forswearing of the joys and satisfactions of family life can at times lead to loneliness, frustration, and pain. Yet these difficulties too are to be offered to the Father by the priest in his life of sacrifice and can add to the perfection of his offering. The priest renounces wife and family precisely because they are so good. The state of celibacy does not reflect negatively on the state of marriage. As Pope John Paul II observed in his apostolic constitution *Familiaris Consortio*, "Virginity or celibacy for the sake of the Kingdom of God not only does not contradict the dignity of marriage but presupposes it and confirms it" (no. 13). As we know, there is no merit in the rejection of evil; however, there *is* merit in forswearing a good out of love for God. The Holy Father quotes St. John Chrysostom to the same effect: "Whoever denigrates marriage also diminishes the glory of virginity. Whoever praises it makes virginity more admirable and resplendent" (no. 14).

THE MARRIED MAN'S SACRIFICE

Marriage is a great good, instituted by God out of love for the crown of His creation, man. Something so beautiful and excellent is renounced only for something more beautiful and excellent still. But as with the priesthood, the real beauty of marriage is seen reflected in the cross. To embrace with abandon and without equivocation the Catholic vocation to marriage is to embrace the cross; it is to enter freely and joyfully into the mystery of Christ's paschal sacrifice; it is to declare one's readiness to sacrifice all for the beloved, even to the point of one's own life.

Familiaris Consortio teaches this very point: "The [revelation of God] reaches its definitive fullness in the gift of love which the Word of God makes to humanity in assuming a human nature, and in the sacrifice which Jesus Christ makes of Himself on the cross for His Bride the Church. In this sacrifice there is entirely revealed that plan which God has imprinted on the humanity of man and woman since their creation, the marriage of baptized persons thus becomes a real symbol of that new and eternal covenant sanctioned in the Blood of Christ" (nos. 10–11). A married couple not only interiorly embrace the cross when they marry, they also show it forth to the Church and the world. "Spouses are therefore the permanent reminder to the Church of what happened on the cross; they are for one another and for their children witnesses to the salvation in which the sacrament makes them sharers" (no. 10).

Although any human life entails suffering, it is not the suffering of Calvary to which marriage gives witness, but rather to the deeper reality even of Calvary's suffering—that is, sacrificial, self-giving love. As Pope John Paul II has stated insightfully, "Looking at it in such a way as to reach its very roots, we must say that the essence and role of the family are in the final analysis specified by love. Hence, the family has the mission to guard, reveal and communicate love, and this is a living reflection of and a real sharing in God's love for humanity and the love of Christ the Lord for the Church, His Bride" (no. 15).

Just as the Catholic vocation to the priesthood is characterized by sacrifice, so is the Catholic vocation to family life. To embrace marriage and family as a faithful Catholic requires a willingness to surrender oneself entirely to that reality and to hold nothing back, just as the priest must do in his vocation. This abandonment to family life manifests three principal characteristics: the indissolubility of the marriage bond, a generous openness to God's gift of life, and service to the world and to the Church. And all of these must be fostered and nurtured, formed and informed, by sacrificial love. When these characteristics are acknowledged and lived, Catholic family life is guaranteed of supernatural fulfillment.

INDISSOLUBILITY

The indissolubility of the marital bond, which provides the bedrock foundation for Catholic family life, requires sacrifice—a notion not at all congenial to the modern, secular, hedonistic mind. Although it is a characteristic of any marriage in the light of natural law, indissolubility has come to be associated today almost exclusively with *Catholic* teaching.

Woody Allen, in his movie *Manhattan*, deals with the fragile nature of human relationships in our modern world. In the role of one of the protagonists, as he strolls through Central Park with the girl he loves, he bemoans the fact that relationships no longer have any permanency to them and remarks ruefully, "The only ones who mate for life anymore are Canada Geese and Catholics."

Unfortunately, we know that that is no longer statistically the case, but even when the Catholic population falters in living this reality, the world knows what the Catholic reality is. But to live this reality means sacrifice; it means a total surrender to the spouse and to the common project of building up a family; it means a setting of the mind and will to exclude the possibility of a dissolution of the relationship, ever, under any circumstances, and thus calls forth a resolve to sacrifice whatever is necessary of one's own to maintain that union. There simply are no other options. I remember being told one time by a woman who was not in the happiest marriage, "I could no more cease being his wife than I could cease being my children's mother."

On the natural plane this indissolubility exists ultimately to serve the good of children. Just as the child before birth needs the womb of his mother for protection and nurture, so as a young child and adolescent he needs the environmental womb of the family. The preservation of the marriage sometimes requires sacrifice on the part of the spouses, but it is embraced for the sake of each other and of the children. As Pope John Paul II has said, "Family communion can be preserved and perfected only through a great spirit of sacrifice" (*Familiaris Consortio*, no. 19). It is the institution of the family that gives meaning to the Church's teaching on marital indissolubility.

On the supernatural plane, the indissolubility of marriage exists as a partaking in the unbreakable covenant Jesus Christ has forged with His Bride, the Church. This, too, manifests the character of sacrifice, because that covenant was effected by, sealed with, and ratified in the blood of Christ. "Christian couples are called to participate truly in the irrevocable indissolubility that binds Christ to the Church, His Bride, loved by Him to the end" (no. 18).

If Catholic spouses in their fidelity to one another do not bear witness to the unconditional and irrevocable sacrificial love of Christ for His Church, who in this world remains to do so? We stand virtually alone in the field, upholding this banner of the truth of Christian marriage, a truth that should be known by all simply through the use of their power of reason. Thank God, Catholics are still able to do so through the gift of His grace. "Just as of old

God encountered His people with a covenant of love and fidelity, so our Savior, the Spouse of the Church, now encounters Christian spouses through the Sacrament of Marriage. He abides with them in order that by their mutual self-giving, spouses will love each other with enduring fidelity, as He loved the Church and delivered Himself up for it" (*Gaudium et Spes*, no. 48). The source of our ability to remain faithful, then, is Christ's sacrifice of love, which binds Him to the Church and us to one another forever.

OPENNESS TO LIFE

The second characteristic of the Catholic vocation to marriage and family is openness to the gift of life. Again, this should be a natural virtue acknowledged by all persons of right reason and good will. The truth of the matter is that in today's world even Catholic laity themselves would be entirely bewildered and led astray on this point were it not for the firm and unwavering voice of the Magisterium, "the one authentic guide for the People of God" (in the words of *Familiaris Consortio*).

If a Catholic fully embraces married life and is open to God's inestimable gift of new life within it, chances are that tremendous sacrifices will be called for. Marriage is basically a vocation to children. The Council tells us that "whenever Christian spouses in a spirit of sacrifice and trust in divine providence carry out their duties of procreation with a generous human and Christian responsibility, they glorify the Creator and perfect themselves in Christ" (no. 50).

The Pope and the Council speak of marriage and family in terms of courage, generosity, surrender, and sacrifice. They do not want to delude the People of God with cheap sentimentality about this holy estate and do not flinch from addressing it for what it is—an occasion for calling forth the greatest and noblest sacrifices of which the human person is capable. To present it as something less would be to render God's People less equipped to make the most of it, less ready to see it as an opportunity for heroism and sanctification through suffering. The popes, out of love for us, have been brutally frank and non-sentimental about the nature of this calling. John Paul II in *Familiaris Consortio* makes the words of Paul VI his own: "To diminish in no way the saving teaching of Christ constitutes an eminent form of charity for souls." One of the most difficult tasks Paul VI ever undertook was the writing of *Humanae Vitae*, but it was out of his eminent love for our souls that he would in no way diminish the saving teaching of Christ, no matter the personal cost and pain to him.

THE SACRIFICES OF PARENTHOOD

Tremendous sacrifices are required of those who embrace the Catholic vocation to marriage and an openness to children; sacrifices just as great as those embraced by men who enter the priesthood. The mother goes so far as to risk her very life fulfilling her vocation. She endures the pain and discomfort of carrying the child in her womb; the distended stomach, the leg cramps, the morning nausea, the stretch-marks on belly and breasts. She suffers incisions, scars, and the shedding of her blood. All of these she bears as proudly as a warrior wears the scars of battle endured out of love for his neighbor and homeland. We are each of us indebted to our mothers for the sacrifices they endured in their vocation to life. The debt is more than we could ever begin to repay. Our mothers have given their blood to bear us, their milk to nourish us, and their tears to save us. Their life is one of sacrificial surrender to their husbands and their children, in union with our Lord's own life of surrender.

The vocation of a Catholic father calls for no less, whether on the battlefield, in the factory, deep in the mines, or in the corporate office. Actuarial tables testify to the shortening of their lives through the rigors of working for their family's welfare. They worry about earning enough to meet their children's needs, to provide them with a range of opportunities. They sometimes take on one, two, three additional jobs to augment the income. They know of the struggles to succeed, the loneliness and temptations of business trips, the fear of unemployment and rejection. But a large, generous family means sacrifice. The pain of a father is deep as he has to watch his son open an envelope on Christmas morning with the picture of a bicycle cut from a catalog and the promise that it will be his as soon as enough money can be saved to purchase it. The pain of a father is deep as he sees the disappointment on his daughter's face when she is told he will miss her Confirmation because of an important business trip. The pain of a father is profound when the family budget will not permit such luxuries as soft drinks, ice cream, or bacon, or when his wife will not entertain in the home because she is embarrassed by the worn condition of its furnishings.

Being generous with the gift of life brings joys beyond words, but they do not come without sacrifice. It seems that the changing of dirty diapers will never end, as it literally stretches on for years. The point is reached where one's greatest desire is for but one full night's uninterrupted sleep without having to walk babies back to sleep, cold-sponge the feverish brow and limbs of a young child, clean up the vomit of another at bedside, or sit awake late at night worrying about the adolescent who had promised to be home two hours earlier. The very evening the father had planned to prepare his presentation for the morning sales meeting is the very night his daughter pleads with him to help her finish her science project, which is due the next day. He helps her until three in the morning and still has to prepare his sales presentation. Such a life is taxing and hard but filled with joyful rewards that surpass words. Such a life is an imitation of Christ, Who endured the cross, despising the shame for the glory that lay ahead.

THE FAMILY IN SERVICE

The fathers of the Second Vatican Council, in *Gaudium et Spes*, tell us that "outstanding courage is required for the constant fulfillment of the duties of this Christian calling: Spouses therefore, will need grace for leading a holy life: they will eagerly practice a love that is firm, generous, and prompt to sacrifice and will ask for it in their prayers" (no. 49). Family life is not easy, and no one knows this truth better than the Catholic Church, the defender, nurturer, and sustainer of the family for centuries. But the rewards and joys of family life are so great that one will eagerly sacrifice anything for it. Family life will be enthusiastically embraced out of love for spouse and children as Christ embraced the cross out of love for His Father and us. As John Paul II said, "the function of transmitting life must be integrated into the overall mission of Christian life as a whole which, without the cross, cannot reach the resurrection. . . . Sacrifice cannot be removed from family life, but must be wholeheartedly accepted if the love between husband and wife is to be deepened and become a source of intimate joy" (*Familiaris Consortio*, no. 34).

The realities of Christian life in general and the marital vocation in particular are so intimately interrelated that they cannot exist independently. The Father is known in the Son, and both are loved in the Spirit. Similarly, the spouse cannot be fully loved but in and through the children; the children cannot be fully loved but in and through the spouse. As is commonly said, the greatest thing a father can do for his children is to love their mother. It is in the home that the moral education of humankind begins, with its opportunities for mutual expressions of sacrificial love.

One aspect of the primary purpose of marriage is the education of the children who have blossomed forth from their parents' love. They are to be educated both for this life and the next.[1] But the education for this life and the next is most adequately provided at the foot of the Cross. The sacrificial love the children see in their parents' relationship with one another and with them provides the guiding model for what will bring true joy and peace in their own lives. The husband will place himself at the service of his wife and children to the point of offering his life for them, just as Christ poured out His life for the Church. The wife, knowing that her husband will be sensitive to her every need, gladly submits herself to him, as the Church is docile to her Lord. The children learn that giving is the essence of human relationships and naturally begin sharing among themselves and preparing gifts for others.

[1] "Human life and its transmission are realities whose meaning is not limited by the horizons of this life only: Their true evaluation and full meaning can only be understood in reference to man's eternal destiny" (*Gaudium et Spes*, no. 51).

It is so true that family life consists of giving and taking. And if the ratio between the two is 90-percent giving and 10-percent taking, it will be a happy, fulfilled home. It is instructive that when *Familiaris Consortio* speaks of the rights and obligations of various members of the family, it does so invariably in terms of sacrificial giving. In the section on the rights and role of women, it states, "Above all it is important to underline the equal dignity and responsibility of women with men. This equality is realized in a unique manner in that reciprocal self-giving by each one to the other and by both to the children which is proper to marriage and the family" (no. 22). In other words, the equality of men and women is preeminently an equality of self-sacrifice.

James Coleman, the late sociologist at the University of Chicago who had specialized in the study of the American family, wrote that in the past, when parents ranked those for whom they were most concerned, it was customary that the children came first, the spouse second, and themselves last. In recent years, however, there has been a shuffling of the priorities, with parents listing themselves first, their spouse second, and their children last. The alarming increase in incidence of divorce and abortion today are clearly fruits of this inverse set of priorities. Professor Coleman stated that this shift in priorities would have more devastating long-term sociological effects in the United States than any other contemporary development of which he was aware.

A family, then, which is strongly fastened together and supported on the foundation of the parents' indissoluble union in Christ and their openness to God's gift of life will be prepared to place itself at the service of the Church and the world. In fact, just as the Church extends our Lord's redeeming sacrifice throughout time and space, so too does the family. By virtue of Baptism, the members of a Catholic family are members of a royal priesthood and are charged with the task of redeeming the world. Just as Christ is encountered in every sacrament, so the world encounters Him in the Catholic Sacrament of Marriage. Jesus Christ has saved the members of the Catholic family and through them works to save the world. The members of the Christian family "not only receive the love of Christ and become a saved community, but they are also called upon to communicate Christ's love to their brethren, thus becoming a *saving* community" (no. 49).

Furthermore, Christian families gather to offer with the priest Christ's redemptive sacrifice in the Mass. Christian families are the source of vocations to the priesthood and the religious life. Christian families are the fields from which doctors, teachers, lawyers, craftsmen, and laborers are harvested, all making their contribution to society. The family fulfills itself by giving itself to the Church and to the world.

MARRIAGE AND PRIESTHOOD — DIFFERENT VOCATIONS

If this total sacrificial abandon is characteristic of the vocation to family life, how can it be combined with the vocation to the priesthood? We know that the two vocations are not essentially incompatible, but they are pretty nearly so in practice. Both the Catholic priest and the Catholic father are called to a life of sacrifice in imitation of Christ. But not imitation simply in the sense of providing a moral example of the type of life Christ led. Their imitation of Jesus means being taken up into Christ's own sacrifice and offering their lives *with His* for the redemption of the world. Their respective states in life mean that the one unique sacrifice of Christ takes on a different configuration in each. But if each lives Christ's sacrifice to the utmost within his respective vocation, it is difficult to imagine living both in one life.

My own former pastoral ministry within the Episcopal Church bore ample illustrations. There were often conflicts between duties to one's natural family and to one's parish family On one occasion I was called to the hospital to baptize a newborn. The baby had meningitis, a highly contagious and potentially deadly disease, and was in an isolation room. I was dressed in gown and mask before being admitted to baptize him. However, just prior to entering, I hesitated. What if I carried the disease home to my own children? What if I contracted the disease myself and deprived my young family of a husband and father? Of course, I baptized the child, but a celibate priest would not have had even to hesitate. He could go anywhere in service to God's children in need without worrying at all about such conflicting obligations.

On another occasion, after becoming a Catholic layman, I was taking care of my sick wife and two of the eight children. My wife was running a very high fever, so I fixed the evening meal, got all the younger children ready for bed, cleaned the house, and helped my daughter with her homework. I finally dropped into bed exhausted at midnight, but was awakened at 2 A.M. by the baby, whose fever had risen. That was the last I slept that night. The remaining hours were spent dispensing aspirin, cleaning up diarrhea, and walking two crying children. My professional duties still awaited me the following morning despite the disruptive night.

When I attended Mass that day the priest apologized for not having prepared a homily. He had been involved in counseling until midnight, he said, at which point he had fallen into bed, dog-tired, only to be roused at 2 A.M. to go to the hospital to minister to a mother whose premature newborn was in danger of death and whose husband was at sea. I thought of my own experiences the previous night and how it would have been impossible for me to have responded as did the priest. And I recognized that the priest had been father to that premature baby and husband to its mother. He was able to bring the grace of the sacraments and the love and encouragement of his ministry into their lives. Because of his priestly celibacy, he was free and able to be spouse, father, friend, and brother to anyone he encountered, in a way in which I could not.

TOTAL VOCATIONS

Both vocations are total. No father would have an unlisted telephone number kept from his children. No priest would do so, either. No father would hesitate to cancel a golf outing if his children needed him. No priest would, either. No husband would dream of not visiting his wife in the hospital. No priest would dream of not visiting a sick parishioner. No husband and father would hesitate to sacrifice all he had for his family's welfare. No priest would hesitate to do the same for his flock.

Presbyterorum Ordinis states that "the priestly soul strives to make its own what is enacted on the altar of sacrifice" (no. 14). The lay person obviously has a lay vocation, but he likewise can carry it out with a priestly soul, making also his own what is enacted on the altar of sacrifice. As *Lumen Gentium* says, "Since He wishes to continue his witness and his service through the laity also, the supreme and eternal Priest, Christ Jesus, vivifies them with

His spirit and ceaselessly impels them to accomplish every good and perfect gift" (no. 34).

Both the Catholic priest and the Catholic family man have the vocation of sharing in Christ's eternal priesthood, but each according to his state. "Christian spouses and parents can and should offer their unique and irreplaceable contribution to the elaboration of an authentic evangelical discernment in the various situations and cultures in which men and women live their marriage and their family life. They are qualified for this role by their charism or specific gift, the gift of the Sacrament of Matrimony" (*Familiaris Consortio*, no. 5).

The priest, in his life and with his charism of celibacy, witnesses to that eschatological age when men and women will no longer be given in marriage. In him, that eschatological age has already broken in upon us. The Catholic couple, on the other hand, witnesses to the way in which marriage should be lived in this world. The Catholic priest witnesses to the beauty of marriage by renouncing it completely out of love for God. The Catholic couple witnesses to the beauty of marriage by embracing it totally, with all its heavy demands, out of love for God.

The Catholic couple witnesses to the proper role of sexuality by using it rationally, placing it at the service of the spouse and of new life. The priest witnesses a life of sacrifice by placing himself entirely at the disposal of his people, and his people at the disposal of the world. The Catholic family witnesses a life of sacrifice as all the members place themselves at the service of one another and the family at the service of the Church and the world (no. 59).

The Catholic priest and the family man have parallel vocations, the priest raising up sons and daughters according to the Spirit, the father according to the flesh and the Spirit.

Its discussion of the priestly vocation of the family occurs in one of the more beautiful passages of *Familiaris Consortio*. "In effect," the document states, "the baptismal priesthood of the faithful exercised in the Sacrament of Marriage constitutes the basis of a priestly vocation and mission for the spouses and family by which their daily lives are transformed into spiritual sacrifices acceptable to God through Jesus Christ." In the domestic church, which is the Catholic family, prayers and sacrifices are constantly offered to God by way of living the life of Christ in the world. "Only by praying together with their children can a father and mother exercising their royal priesthood—penetrate the innermost depths of their children's hearts and leave an impression that the future events in their lives will not be able to efface" (no. 60). The "royal priesthood" of the family is exercised *not* by doing clerical things, but by being a family, by doing those things proper to family life.

The family in its own unique way bears witness to Christ's sacrificial love. While the priest bears graphic witness to the next world by renouncing so many of the goods of this one, the family is fully integrated into this world, drawing attention to its true goods, properly regarded. The mother at the poolside watching her children play in the water on a summer's afternoon bears Christian witness to the young woman sitting on the grass beside her, in a way in which a priest never could. The father taking his son and one of his son's friends sailing or rabbit-hunting can bear witness to the Christian role of a father to the other boy's father in a manner in which a priest never could. This is what *Apostolicam Actuositatem* (Decree on Lay People) calls the "apostolate of like to like."

> The apostolate in one's social environment endeavors to infuse the Christian spirit into the mentality and behavior, laws and structures of the community in which one lives. To such a degree is it the special work and responsibility of lay people, that no one else can properly supply it for them (no. 13).

As Catholics, we live in the temporal, as well as in the eternal, order; and "laymen ought to take on themselves as their distinctive task [the] renewal of the temporal order" (no. 7). The family is the principal means of our insertion into society and the means through which we laity make our witness to the world. "The mission of being the primary vital cell of society has been given to the family by God Himself" (no. 11). As such, and ideally, all social relationships (and the virtues that regulate them) have their source in the family.

The Church has always borne witness to the primacy of the family as the basic social unit. Relationships within the Church are patterned after familial relationships. Even the common language of the Church illustrates this patterning. Priests are addressed as Father, Religious as Brother and Sister, women religious superiors as Mother. It is no accident that the counter-faith of our world would reject titles drawn from "outdated" social institutions like the family, and would substitute instead "Comrade," a title that denies distinctions between male and female and the natural hierarchy of relationships existing in the family.

Everyone within the Body of Christ is called to holiness,

each according to one's own state. The path to sanctity requires total abandonment and an embracing of the redeeming cross of Christ. The wild abandon characteristic of the committed Catholic allows for no compromise. It remembers with dread the words of our Lord, "You are neither hot nor cold; therefore, I will vomit you out of my mouth" (Rev 3:13). Each vocation, the priestly, the religious, and the lay, is glorious, and each calls for the totality of the person. In the words of G. K. Chesterton, "It *is* true that the historic Church has at once emphasised celibacy and emphasised the family; has at once (if one may put it so) been fiercely for having children and fiercely for not having children. It has kept them side by side like two strong colors, red and white, like the red and white upon the shield of St. George. It has always had a healthy hatred of pink." [2]

[2] G. K. Chesterton, *Orthodoxy* (1924), chap. 6.

Why I'm Not Celibate—But Glad That Catholic Priests Are!

REVEREND DAVID HARTMAN

What kind of *chutzpah* does it take for a married Protestant minister to expound on priestly celibacy? For that's what I am—a member of the Protestant cloth, married, the father of three children. I'm tickled with my wife and delighted with my kids, I don't have to take cold showers or avoid eating oysters, and my back is always warm at night. For those reasons and others, the recurring request of some Catholic priests for that which has been a given for Protestant clergy—permission to marry and procreate—strikes a powerful personal chord.

But my point in writing is not to say "Nyaah, nyaah, nyaah" to the celibates, but instead to say (to the extent that a non-celibate has any authority at all in the matter) that clerical celibacy is probably a pretty good idea—maybe even a holy one. After over a decade in the ordained ministry, I have reached the unexpected conclusion that there is a compelling case to be made for the disciplined separation of the clerical and the marital vocation. One can serve and honor God in both, of course; but human frailty intrudes. For what we have in the familial and the clerical offices are competing goods. The joining—or rather, the forced fusion of the two does not produce a single greater good. Instead—and here I *can* speak with authority—such a fusion diminishes one or both. For at some point almost every married member of the clergy must make a decision: To which of my vows—the one to my office or the one to my spouse—do I owe the greater allegiance? A few, no doubt gifted with extraordinary grace, can honor both simultaneously. Most, I think, do not. Implicitly, the deal is struck: I will sacrifice one on the altar of the other.

I know about these major options. In the first, the internal covenant goes: "My ministry matters more to me than my marriage, and my wife must accommodate herself to that fact." St. Peter may have been the greatest apostle of them all, but the New Testament record of this peripatetic disciple doesn't portray a prize-winner among husbands. And what of the wife who is married to a cleric who gets his jollies from public acclaim instead of at home? Sometimes, she will suffer in silence and sublimate her unhappiness by trying to live up to the degrading, time-hallowed fantasy of what a Preacher's Wife ought to be—sweet, helpful, never ubiquitous but always ready to pitch in when a potluck dinner needs overseeing or the Church School needs superintending.

One of the pastoral-care horror stories I picked up at seminary was about an institutionalized wife of a Presbyterian minister. Six days of the week, she went from patient to patient and asked, "Can I help you? Is there anything you need?" On Sundays she flew into such violent rages that she had to be restrained and sedated. Meanwhile, the sympathies of the congregation, of course, were largely with her long-suffering, saintly spouse, whose halo gleamed more grandly because of his fidelity to a looney. Not all the spouses of plaster saints wind up with a life full of lithium, of course. Sometimes a spouse will decide she has had enough and fill up her life with her own work; sometimes she will just fax her husband the name and number of her attorney.

In most evangelical and fundamentalist Protestant churches, a divorce is the kiss of vocational death. No doubt this fact plays a great part in the lower incidence of divorce among conservative preachers; it hardly contributes to the exhilaration of marital *eros*. Among more liberal Protestant churches, where clerical divorce is absolved with ready benediction of "Such a tragedy!", the dissolution of a marriage rarely results in a compulsory exit from the ministry, unless there is blatant adultery involved (and sometimes not even then). But it nonetheless sends a powerful message to laity, who may be looking to the pastor as an example of how seriously they ought to take their own marriage vows. A seminary professor I know says that whenever a parish minister divorces, there tends to be an immediate and corresponding increase in divorces among members of the congregation. "It gives them permission," he says.

The reverse is also true. There are ministers who place their marriage vows over those of their ordination. I put myself in this category. I have promised my wife that if the ministry is ever irredeemably destructive to our marriage, I will leave the ministry—which means that my ordination vows, which I took with such seriousness, have been moved to secondary status among the promises I intend to keep. A few times she has come perilously close to cashing in that chip, notably when, half an hour after the birth of our second son, I left their sides to attend a wedding rehearsal. Those priceless few hours after birth, when the bond between parent and newborn is initiated, were lost because of what I thought was an inescapable *vocation* responsibility.

When family vacations have been cut short because of an emergency in the congregation; when a long-promised

bike ride with my son is forsaken because a desperate parishioner calls to say *her* son is in trouble; when the com-
plaints of a critical parishioner reach my wife because of
something I have either done or failed to do—on such
occasions (which I could expand upon *ad infinitum*) the
particular manifestations of the Body of Christ I serve no
longer seem redemptive but ravenous. This is the case even
though the congregation I serve has been generous, gentle,
and forgiving. (A note: At the very moment I finished
composing the preceding sentence, a member called: Her
sister's husband died. Can I come? Of course. They are my
friends; this is my vocation. My wife understands. She will
put the children to bed herself. She is used to it.)

For all my congregation's goodness of heart, however,
there is an implicit expectation on the part of many that my
family will somehow be immune from the common plagues
of family life. We will not be angry at one another in public;
our children (being Preacher's Kids) are expected to be
mischievous, but not annoying; the lawn of the parsonage
will stay kempt, even if the elves have to take care of it.

I am mindful that all this must seem narcissistic or self-
serving; that I am operating under the delusion that I am
indispensable to the congregation, or that being a local
minister is an unending crown of thorns. Yet, when one
commits to a vocation such as the ministry, does one say
that the job has a statute of limitations—that between 6
P.M. and 8 A.M. one is a civilian? (One certainly would not
say that between 8 A.M. and 6 P.M. one ceases to be married.) And at what point did my wife and children, so
powerfully affected by my ordination vows, take them
themselves? One can say, of course, that other vocations—
medicine, law enforcement, the military, politics—have the
same kinds of demands. But in what other vocation does a

wife have to feel as if she is competing with the Bride of Christ for her husband's affections?

If a pastor cares about the sheep of his flock, he will be perpetually draining himself emotionally. After you have wept with those who mourn one too many times, the well of compassion temporarily runs dry. And if, during those times, your own flesh and blood—those who ought to be most entitled to your care—try to drink from that well? They will go away parched. Of course, one can try to pull off an emotional juggling act—which is what I think most Protestant clergy try to do—caring some here, caring some there, fully investing oneself in neither vocation, fully caring for none. The empowering strength of the Holy Spirit is real, to be sure; but it is not always *felt*.

This is not to say that there are no pluses. When my first son was born, I understood for the first time the meaning of unconditional love. When he turned two, I finally comprehended the doctrine of original sin. Within the confines of my family, I have received mortal intimations of God's grace, patience, and mercy.

Perhaps the two terms so perpetually bandied about on the nature of God—transcendence vs. immanence—can be applied to marriage as well. Lovable folk like Bill Cosby and Garrison Keillor can write with wit and profundity about the *immanent* qualities of family life. They can portray, in ways that ring true, its perplexities and joys. Yet, a pope can speak *transcendently* about marriage, as John Paul II did during an address to the bishops of Cincinnati and Detroit in 1988, when he called marriage "a vocation to holiness." Earl Butz's Neanderthal gibe about papal encyclicals on birth control—"He no play-a da game, he no make-a da rules"—betrays an unlettered assumption that those who look down from a mountaintop have no authority to speak about the valley below. And I do not think it coincidental that Catholicism, which exalts and hallows marriage far above its mainline Protestant counterparts, has a clergy which, except with rare dispensations, is celibate. My friend Sheldon Vanauken recently wrote, "Both matrimony and ordination are sacraments. . . . Both matrimony and ordination are forever,[1] altering the soul. That does not mean—the Church would not say—that one must exclude the other. Unlike the doctrinal requirement of a male priesthood, a celibate priesthood is but a rule, a discipline." He's absolutely right, of course, about celibacy being a discipline rather than a doctrine; and the reason for a rule (if it be a just one) is that it have redemptive ends, or at least redemptive results.

Perhaps I can, with great humility and the pained awareness that I may not know whereof I speak, suggest one of *this* rule's redemptive results. From the perspective of a married father and cleric, here it is: Only those who have not been married can sustain a transcendent vision of the Sacrament of Marriage, or those who, like Vanauken in his book *A Severe Mercy*, are looking back from the perspective of bereavement. For these can still exalt marriage—can still discern its invisible, transcendent sacredness. To be married and have children—to change dirty diapers, to stay up all night with ear infections, to meet in conference with sorely-annoyed school principals, to howl about the phone bill, to be nearly berserk from exhaustion—*and still try to honor marriage for the sacrament it is*—is to know, however insensibly, the immanent quality of marriage. But something else—a vision of its transcendent nature—may fall by the wayside, perhaps never to be reclaimed except

---

[1] Editor's note: Mr. Vanauken is a bit imprecise here—the Sacrament of Matrimony is not "forever" but "until death do us part."

through bereavement. For Vanauken, darkness and death were, through God's "severe mercy," transformed into light and life. But the transcendent vision returned only after the poignant loss of the immanence, and then only through the gentling grace of distance. He touched on this in *Under the Mercy*, a sequel: "*A Severe Mercy* was the result of years of examining what had been with [my wife] Davy, until with distance foothills sank into the plain and the essential mountains stood forth."

I pray Vanauken's forgiveness if I am using his words to state an opinion he may not hold, but it seems to me that the Church's doctrine of the marital sacrament at least implies that any believer may sense the immanence of marriage—its foothills—while the Church's discipline of clerical celibacy at least suggests that her priests may, without the *via media* of bereavement, still envision its transcendence, its "essential mountains."

There is another consideration, one that may not be so obvious in settled times and places, but one apparent when Christians are called to resist with courage a manifest evil. Children are "hostages to destiny"—that is, their well-being is directly related to the actions of their parents. This is figuratively true whatever the external circumstances. But in those times when evil seems enthroned—as in Nazi Germany, as in the corrupting and murderous power of the Medellin drug cartel in Colombia—children are *literal* hostages, a fact not lost on the wicked, who have no qualms about terrorizing parents with threats against their children. An individual who may be stalwart if his or her own life is the only one in jeopardy is much more likely to be quiescent if the lives of loved ones are in jeopardy, as well. In describing the response of the German churches to Nazism, Ferdinand Friedensburg, a gallant Protestant pastor who was imprisoned because of his opposition to Hitler, noted: "The Catholic Church [has] been... in a different, somewhat more favorable situation.... [Its] clergymen were less exposed to blackmail and bribery than their Protestant brothers, since celibacy gave them no wives and children for whom they had to care."

In times when the Church is called to be prophetic—authentically prophetic, as opposed to the constitutionally protected rhetoric that passes for prophecy in our day—priestly celibacy may be the single greatest contributing factor to a courageous pastoral witness.

Of course, celibacy is an aberration—an aberration because of the normal human drive to mate and procreate. It is, in its own way, as much of an aberration as a soldier throwing himself on a grenade to save the lives of his buddies, or God dying on a cross. In other words, celibates who are celibate for the sake of the Church are engaged in a lifelong act of self-denial. One might even say that those who are celibate for the sake of their priestly vocations are heroic. For is there not something heroic in anyone who surrenders his life in such an extraordinary way for such invisible, transcendent ends?

There are, of course, compensations. For example, I have come to understand that while celibacy is a disciplined denial of the sexual act, it is not a denial of one's sexuality, which is as much a part of one's wholeness as a whole body and mind. I have a friend—a nun in her fifties, a woman of singularly delightful personality. She has a friend—an English priest in his fifties—who makes a pilgrimage every couple of years just to be in her company. Whenever I see them together—talking, arguing, walking in silence through the park—it is obvious that she delights in his manhood, as he does in her womanhood; but neither violates, nor (I trust) would consider violating, his or her vows. In their holy denial of one aspect implicit in a relationship between a man and a woman, they seem to have discovered the deep fountains of joy implicit in all the rest.

Clerical Marriage from a Wife's Viewpoint

JESSICA MILLARD HARTMAN

Marriages and ordinations are both acts performed upon God's altar, and for good reason. Altars are traditionally used for making sacrifices. The priest taking vows at ordination knows he is making a personal sacrifice for the good of the Body of Christ. Neither the bride and groom taking vows on their wedding day nor the priest at his ordination can possibly know what sacrifices will be required of them in keeping the vows they make before God. God's grace proves completely necessary for the undertaking of either commitment. Each vow requires total dedication and complete devotion. Many marriages fail because of the intensity of the required sacrifice.

Marriage requires total sacrifice for the benefit of the man and the woman and the children born of this particular union. In ordination, the priest-minister commits himself to be married, in a way, to the Bride of Christ, the Church. This "marriage" requires a similar commitment to the souls under the care of the priest. In marriage, a minister commits himself to one woman. Both commitments require God's assistance, because neither commitment can be kept apart from the grace of God.

Sinful human beings take on these commitments without knowing where they will lead or what they will cost, but trusting God with the details of life and death. The need to preserve one's self is strong, and the will to make daily sacrifices remains, well, weak. The miraculous quality of marriage is that at times it does succeed. Sometimes married couples grasp heavenly joy in their communion with one another, and, in their mutual task, they begin to see the heavenly kingdom at work within the sacred bonds of their own precious family.

Satan must work overtime to see to it that families never get a glimpse of heaven. Once heaven can be seen within a family, no one in that family would dream of settling for any cheap imitation. Families so sanctified are so rare and so valuable. Families that grasp a vision of God's kingdom provide light to a dark world. Other souls in need of grace often find comfort among these blessed families. Because through such marriages their needs are always met "according to God's riches in glory," they always have time and wealth to spare, nurturing the souls around them. Families built upon the love and grace of God are able to face whatever comes, knowing that God's kingdom is not of this world, but that the rewards for any sacrifice made for the glory of God more than make up for any temporary sacrifice or inconvenience. Souls given such a vision of the heavenly realm will protect it with all their strength and will not allow anything to divert attention from the truth of God's love and compassion for all the world.

Jesus compares the kingdom of heaven to a treasure buried in a field. This treasure is passed on through the generations by parents in homes whose commissions are given at God's altar in the Sacrament of Matrimony. When marriage fails, the treasure goes undiscovered. Marriage protects and defends the whole family from all the evils of this world. Functioning families show the whole world how to enter into God's kingdom in joy. Parents guide children into full participation in the joy of the fellowship of the Holy Spirit, first because of the joys of life within the intimacy of the family. Souls are naked before God, and the truth of human souls is exposed within the family God gives. Families know one another's strengths and weaknesses: no dishonesty allowed. Families tease and chide one another into being better people and facing life with the knowledge that there are people who will take your part and defend you from evil at great cost. No one can reasonably claim that he or she arrived fully formed and ready to take on the world without first entering into some form of a family and forming a personality in the intimacy of that relationship.

Even the Father deemed it necessary to place Jesus within a human family. God could certainly have formed Jesus in much the same way Adam was formed and placed into the garden of Eden. Instead, we are presented with a whole cast of characters from which Jesus formed His own human identity. Jesus has Mary and Joseph, blessed by a visit from an angel, yet left to accomplish their marriage and parenthood in real time and in real sacrifice. Even the most ardent skeptics do not doubt the sacrifices made by Mary and by Joseph.

Jesus also has extended family in Elizabeth, Zechariah, and John. Elizabeth's husband, Zechariah, too, is startled by the appearance of an angel, yet the couple must do their work in earthly circumstances. John may be conceived by a special act of God, but his personality and faith are formed in his all-too-human family. This family conspired to build God's kingdom on earth as it is in heaven. John knows heaven so well from his own experience that he gives up all hope of earthly comfort in adulthood to clear the way for his second cousin to give His life for the sins of the whole world. This sacrifice remains inexplicable apart from the heavenly cause that Elizabeth and Zachariah embrace within their holy marriage. Notice, too, that John is nurtured in a priestly family. God lived in the family, and His presence was a reality within the walls of their homes. The whole enterprise seems completely irrational without knowledge of God and heaven. The treasure of heaven makes more sense than the pleasures of earth only because John is grounded in the love of God and the fellowship of the Holy Spirit from his infancy and in his own God-given family. Character is formed within the crucible of the family.

Christianity is a religion based upon a Holy Family. Human children learn to be members of Christ's Body through membership in a very private club, committed to one another by the most intimate of bonds. A real family will operate like the Three Musketeers, in an all-for-one and one-for-all unity. The family is composed of some of the oddest creatures you will ever encounter. First of all, a man marries a woman, and if one recent author on the subject is correct (and many people agree that he is), men and women hail from separate planets and approach the world in radically different ways. Who says that God lacks a sense of humor? What seems terribly important to the woman doesn't even rate a mention on the man's radar screen, and many of the real concerns of a man may cause a woman to yawn in boredom. The holiness of the family may appear somewhere in the compromise necessary to meet the needs of both husband and wife, and let us not forget the children.

The children arrive with competing needs and goals and separate personalities, and they must come to terms with each other. Children vie for parental love and affection and compete with one another to make an impression upon the world they did not choose, but a world in which God chose them and gave them their own quirky place in it.

God forms families and then requires these aliens to work together to solve problems of increasing difficulty, something like a television show in which a group of strangers is taken to a desert island and told to fend for themselves. The one saving grace for this band of strangers is that they may weekly vote someone off the island. This option is a temptation too for all of us who live in families. When one member becomes tedious or difficult or burdensome, we are sorely tempted to "vote" him or her out of the family. However, the rules of Christianity do not allow this option. The real game of marriage and family is far tougher than television fantasies, because we are never allowed to vote another soul off this island. The stakes are far too high. When the covenant of marriage is broken, Humpty Dumpty might not be put back together again.

When a clergyman marries, one covenant feeds into another. He is responsible to give his life for the welfare of the wife, and then for the welfare of the children. He also is responsible to give his life for the welfare of the flock under his care, which includes his own wife and children, and sometimes he may blur the difference between them and the rest of the congregation. This blurring of distinctions can be deadly, not only for the family of the minister, but for the congregation, as well. Once the wife and children begin to blend into the flock, they may become the lost sheep.

A woman who marries a minister soon notices something very strange is happening. All the occasions that mark the life of most families are, in her case, carried on in the absence of her husband. He tends the flock during the times when the other families are not working (Christmas, Easter, Thanksgiving, weekends, other holidays). Christmas Eve will find the pastor trying to write a hurried sermon. Never mind that the "text" for Christmas never changes. We always have the Babe in the manger, the shepherds, the angelic chorus singing the first Christmas carol in the *Gloria*, assorted Wise Men from the East, and some sort of profound statement upon the nature of the Incarnation. The minister struggles to present Christmas to the flock while the flock merrily enjoys the Christmas holiday with their own families and friends. Children of the minister remember Daddy pecking away at the keys of the computer rather than gathering the family to read St. Luke and participating in the lighting of the Christmas tree in their home. He faithfully assembles various members of the congregation to light the candles for the church, but often fails to appear for similar rituals in his own home. Obviously he is "ritualled out." So is his poor family. The family becomes expert at preparing potluck dishes and eating fried chicken, but seldom participates in the usual family dinner-table banter detailing daily trials and joys. Absent time devoted to family, the family drifts, and the shoemaker's children do go without shoes. The consequences for the family of doing without fathering prove deadly.

The strains on the family of a cleric creep up on it. In efforts to imitate Jesus and to represent the unity between Christ and His Church, the family of the clergyman begins to develop cracks in its integrity. Every sin must be glossed over, and any imperfection must be absorbed rather than faced and confessed. When trouble arises, there is nowhere to turn. Even retreats set up to minister to the ministers fall far short of their stated goal.

When our marriage was on the brink of total dissolution, my husband and I attended a retreat for ministers and their spouses. Meetings were held in which the ministers, both male and female, were seated at tables around the room along with seminarians. The wives who were still "game" for attending these events with their spouses were seated in a corner away from any center of attention and given topics to discuss among themselves. This exclusion from the center of life is typical for the family of the minister, because it protects the family from being exposed in what is rarely a perfect situation and allows for the continuation of the fiction that the family lives in complete bliss and communion with the Holy Spirit. The wives notice that when other clergy-couples fail in their marriages, the wives simply disappear. The ministers in such cases seldom remain single for long; they simply find another woman to take the place of the previous wife, moving to another church and another community to repent publicly of their sins, forming a new family and a new fiction with a new woman. The church has come to accept this as normal. No one even looks to see what might have happened to the former family of this "saint" who repents so publicly. He forgives himself and leaves all the baggage behind.

When my marriage blew up into a million pieces beneath the strains of public hypocrisy and private anguish, my husband had the integrity to offer his resignation as spokesperson for the risen Christ. Fortunately or unfortunately, as the case may be, the congregation rallied to his side and insisted that he remain as their minister. This meant a whole community was taking sides against his family and feeling extremely sorry for him—his wife didn't understand his sainthood.

Our children suffered under the strain of their mother's public shunning. My husband and I were separated and then divorced for nearly three years before the wounds we had each committed against one another in the marriage healed enough for us even to consider reconciliation with one another. When reconciled, it was with a commitment to live an honest life before God and man and not to participate in any hypocritical fiction that is forced upon the family of a minister. We were not and are not perfect. Our marriage was not and is not perfect. Our children are sinful human beings who, like us, make errors in judgment from time to time. We live as sinners in a sinful world and seek God's forgiveness for our many transgressions.

In the case of the minister, to deny the family time and attention because he works preparing "meaningful experiences" for others eventually reaps what is sown, and the family sees itself as missing a member. The minister eventually finds himself voted off the island. The family goes on with whatever needs to be done; if the minister does not devote time and attention to his own family, he might come home to find that he is no longer expected or even wanted.

Time is the treasure of life. When Jesus says, "Where your treasure is, there will your heart be also," He is speaking quite literally. Wherever you put time, toil, and tears, you have invested all you have to give. Priests give their lives to Christ's Church, and that is fitting. Most wives of ministers are at peace with the notion of having godly men for husbands, and ministers seldom marry women who are not supportive of this vocation. Godliness is not always the result. Ministers are given to self-sacrifice, or they would not choose to be ministers in the first place. So, too, their wives. This results in marriage between two people who might not consider each other's needs until they find themselves suffocating under an unbearable burden of personal neglect.

When the minister fails to tend to the needs of his wife and vice versa, the fabric of family life can be strained to the breaking point. Unless they both develop some deep reserve of love and affection for one another, they can easily drift apart and seek solace outside the marriage covenant. This does not have to mean adultery. This can mean even seemingly good works that keep the two from spending the necessary time to know that the treasure is spent in the relationship and not outside of it. This becomes very difficult within the ministry because the husband is covenantally committed to two very different callings. Often the mundane problems of hearth and home have less appeal than the general adoration often mis-bestowed upon the man of the cloth. Having a father who is universally admired and appreciated causes a negative effect on the children who find it difficult to live up to the perfection they are told is represented by their father. Children see most clearly the weaknesses of parents. Families of clergymen find themselves fielding countless compliments for the clergyman. "You are so fortunate to have such a wonderful father," someone says, with no idea what kind of a father the man may be. Usually the wife and children are not taken as separate individuals or appreciated for any contributions they might make. Anything the children do for the church is simply expected, and any triumph they may experience reflects more upon the father than upon themselves, while any faults are amplified as unworthy of his children.

Many people assign God-like qualities to the minister and tempt him to believe extraordinary things about himself. His family has his number, however, and will not necessarily adore him in the same way. It is much easier for him to find avenues of escape from the truth of life at home than to come home and face the music with people who are aware of his faults. These people who make up his family are the ones who may truly love him, not as the icon that is the minister of the congregation, but as the husband and father.

The family of a clergyman often faces untold criticism from the rest of the congregation. When conflict arises between members of the congregation and his wife, more than one minister has been known to side with the members rather than with his wife. Thus he is saved the embarrassment of watching his wife have any conflict with any saintly church member.

My own marriage ended for me the day a member went to my husband to tell him that I was mentally ill and should be put under medical treatment immediately. In the midst of the whole debacle, my husband forgot completely that his role as my husband was to defend me, as Christ defends and advocates for me at the throne of God, even if I am wrong, which I often am. My trust in my husband had been broken, and from there our marriage fell apart. That episode was not the first such time; it was the straw that broke the camel's back of our relationship.

Other problems plague a clerical family. The family appears regularly in church, but the family of the pastor does not actually go to church *with* the pastor, or anywhere else for that matter. He can always be found meeting and greeting about town; but even if he takes his family out to dinner, he is seldom left alone to visit with them. The clergyman husband and father keeps a watchful eye on the children to make sure that they do not provide any embarrassment to himself.

Once, our son left the church service, climbed to the top floor onto the roof with a friend, and proceeded to scale the elevator shaft, which was under construction. The temperature was 15 degrees, the snow was blowing, the roof was iced over, and the winds were raging at fifty miles an hour. No one in his right mind would have conceived such a scheme. A church member spotted him and coaxed him into the building. Herein lies the real problem for the minister: a member of his family might conceive a hair-brained scheme and carry it out under his nose and during his sermons. While he is delivering a sermon with great solemnity, he finds that he has lost the family he brought with him—and *they* may be found dangling from the elevator shaft. There is no togetherness achieved for the minister's family during worship. The family is not together. While other families may be holding hands and giving each other kind looks during a church service and sometimes thinking kind thoughts about one another, the family of the clergyman may scatter in other directions, bored from the sheer repetition of the proceedings. The truth of the Gospel may be completely lost on them as they see their father and husband giving a kind of performance week after week. Since the minister is appreciated by the congregation for his work and idolized by his many fans, it is easy to see why he might not want to come home from being among his many admirers. It takes a strong person indeed to see that flattery is only flattery, and not reality.

The effect is doubled if the same father rarely makes an appearance at home, except to grab an occasional bite to eat or to sleep. If the minister returns home only when he is exhausted or in need of solace, he may eventually find that there is no solace in returning home. If some of his time is not invested in the home and family, then the treasure that might be found there and given away there will never materialize, and the children will never have the benefit of knowing their father as a real father, and not simply as a clergyman.

I once asked my daughter what it was like for her to live

with a minister as a father. She replied that it was like missing one family member. She loves her father, and he loves her. Her father and I have long since patched up our differences and re-committed our lives to one another, but the problem of not serving two masters is still with us, and sometimes the family still gets the short end of the ministerial stick.

If ministers are to be married, and if the work of the Holy Spirit is to continue, more energy must be expended on aiding these families and all the families of Christ's Church to understand the sacrifice and the joy of marriage, and to honor the treasure to be found within the covenant of marriage.

Until such time, I shall struggle on as the wife of a minister, but I am also deeply appreciative of the wisdom and sensitivity of the Catholic Church's position whereby neither the covenant of priesthood nor the covenant of marriage must exist in tension and competition with each other.

Priestly Celibacy in the Light of Medicine and Psychology

WANDA POLTAWSKA

Unlike celibacy for lay people, the celibacy of the priest is determined by the free and conscious choice made by a psychically mature man (it is one of the main conditions put to anyone wishing to take Holy Orders) and as such does not cause a sense of frustration. This frustration, however, is a very common psychological reaction among single lay people who would like to get married but cannot, and so feel "condemned" to a life of loneliness. Reactions of this sort are more common in women than in men, and in many cases the ungratified desire for married life and motherhood gives rise to bouts of psychic depression.

Making a choice always means giving up other possibilities, other values, but a free choice willingly made also bears witness to the conviction that the value chosen is superior to all the other ones. The priesthood is so charged with potential for self-realization as to give the life of the man who has chosen it a sense of fullness that is often lacking in the lives of ordinary people. Spiritual fatherhood, the power to bind and loose, the joy of bearing, with his own hands, the supreme gift of God Himself to others: these place the priestly dignity on so high a plane in the hierarchy of human possibilities that it cannot be compared with anything else whatsoever and leaves no room for frustration.

As most people see it, the priest is bound forever to the obligation of celibacy, and, generally speaking, this disposition of the Church has hardly been challenged in past centuries. The vocation to the priesthood and the vocation to marriage both require the same total devotion and hence are mutually exclusive, even though the type of personality required is basically the same in both cases. At this moment in history, however, we do not so much have a repudiation of the actual ideal of celibacy as doubt about the real possibility of sticking to decisions connected with it.

When John Paul II speaks of priestly celibacy, he often qualifies it as "sacred"—"sacred priestly celibacy"—emphasizing that it is not simply a matter of renouncing married life, for its deep significance lies in chastity and virginity, in supreme union with God.

Celibacy and the sixth commandment

Because of the growing tendency to permissiveness and the exaltation of the biological dimension of human nature, the modern world tends to deny people's ability to live chastely throughout their lives. By some people, the renunciation of sexual activity is perceived as a punishment, by others as an unattainable ideal, by yet others as a way of life that is "against human nature."

Forgetting the special grace of the sacrament, which affords the support and strength needed for fulfilling such a vocation, people often confuse priestly celibacy with the celibacy of lay people who, having no deep motivation, do not keep the sixth commandment, even though considering themselves believing Catholics. The law laid down by God and intended for everyone "not to fornicate," they also question on the basis of what they see going on every day around them. So many people transgress this commandment today that it might well seem "unsuited" to human capacities, as though it were impossible to observe it.

This increasingly widespread permissive ethics has given rise to an attitude of expectation of a definite change in the teaching of the Church, not only over priestly celibacy but indeed over all standards and, among others, over the obligations of the sixth commandment. Seeking from purely pastoral motives to help the people of today, whose specific life-style is largely governed by conceptions of comfort, the Church has already relaxed certain rules of conduct, and this has aroused expectation of further changes, especially as regards questions whose definition pertains to the ecclesiastical authorities and is not directly derived from Divine Revelation.

Since priestly celibacy, introduced on the basis of experience, has intrinsically the nature of human and not divine decision, the people of the present day seem to be waiting for "something to change." This attitude of uncertainty, of the "open door," makes respect for chastity even harder, even on the part of priests. Now, the final and unequivocal decision—"I choose celibacy once and forever, beyond all hope of recall"—like all unequivocal and final decisions, is easier to fulfill than an uncertain one—"Perhaps I will, but we'll see about that—later"—which encourages the sin of fornication by weakening the mechanism of self-control needed for keeping the sixth commandment. There is a fairly general conviction that the only cure for the problems connected with celibacy would be to allow the clergy to get married. For the frequency with which fornication is committed raises doubts over the real possibility of living according to other models. Modern people often forget that the sixth commandment applies to everyone without exception, and that no circumstances exist that can suspend the validity of this divine law.

The question next arises whether the abolition of celibacy

should simply constitute permission to contract indissoluble marriage, or rather lead to a demand for the introduction of the right to a sex life independent of marriage, that is to say, basically, an attempt to sanction fornication in general, and even for priests. The growing tendency to recognize the "rights" of the young to sexual activity often means that preparation for the sacrament of marriage, as also for the priesthood, will have been preceded by "presacramental" fornication, whether of hetero- or homosexual type. Experiences of this sort, to some degree, condition the behavior of the person and leave an imprint, a memory, which will later make control of the individual's own reactions even harder.

THE FALSE CONCEPTION OF SEXUALITY

The permissive sexual ethics of today originates in a false conception of human sexuality in general. The fact of being endowed with sex, which makes human reproduction possible, does not make the sex act necessary *per se*. We are not programmed as to our sexual activity; in the human organism there exist no mechanisms forcing us to act in this way. The only thing determined is sexuality, the Creator's gift, transmitted by our parents at our first instant of life. The whole somatic structure and psychic development of the human being are closely connected with sex as they develop; human existence, in every one of its aspects, bears the features of sexuality; everything we achieve in the course of our lives is marked by it. Hence, sexuality is a way of existing in the world, and it is, therefore, absolutely wrong to speak of it as something separate from the human entity: sex as such, as an abstract concept separate from us, does not exist. Only the human being exists, endowed with sexuality: unable to shed our own sexuality, we are male or female, as the case may be, throughout our lives. The whole human body bears the features of this innate sexuality and is subject to a complex nervous system and biological functions that are independent of our will. The human organism, the supreme work of the Creator, is in its complexity a very harmonious whole, ordered with a fascinating precision independent of the subject. Without being commanded by the human will, the body of its own accord follows the laws of its own nature: all the reactions occurring in the organism in the course of its entire life-cycle come from God and are His gift.

Endowed with all the organs needed for living, the human body also possesses those, improperly called sexual, which are, however, essentially procreative, their function being to pass on the gift of life. By endowing us with these organs, the Creator has granted us the opportunity of collaborating with Him in the great work of creation.

In collaboration of this sort, the human person is called by God to the Sacrament of Marriage, which unites husband and wife in accordance with the divine plan—"they will be two persons in a single body"—on which the physiological structure of the human organism depends. But not all of us are called to be parents: some of us have other tasks to discharge. The call to reproduce, even though frequent, is not common to all. Sexuality, as a characteristic of the individual, is given to each of us; but procreation is the task only for those who have been called to it by the Creator.

THE MYTH OF ORGASM

The sexual act uniting husband and wife needs some stimulus to the sexual organs, for these normally remain inactive. A person with normal reactions does not feel any particular excitement of a sexual nature unless it is induced. The concept of sexual instinct, with reference to human beings, is therefore rather imprecise: in the literal sense of the term, such an instinct does not exist; only certain sexual reactions exist that the human being can go along with but can also control and curb. To be performed, the sex act needs an initial state of excitement, as is easily observed, especially in the male organism. This excitement, which may be caused by an impulse of physiological, emotional, or volitional type, is not only easy to achieve but is also perceived as a pleasurable sensation. The culminating point, known as orgasm, is only the final mechanism for effecting procreation. It makes fertilization easier, even though, obviously, it does not determine it. But orgasm, being a particularly intense and deeply-felt sensation, often becomes the only objective; it becomes divorced from its reproductive function, all the more so since it is considered to be a "sign" of the love with which the actual sex act is often mistakenly identified.

People today yearn for pleasure and look for it wherever they can. Modern sexology gives precise descriptions of different methods for achieving orgasm and of the techniques for causing it, often overlooking the fact that this state of maximum excitement is only a means and not an end, and that it can give rise to conception and all the problems associated with the role of parenthood. The hedonistic attitude puts orgasm among the most desired objectives at which human beings can aim. By the sheer fact of being endowed with sex, human beings feel somehow authorized to be sexually active, sometimes even claiming to be forced to be so by their own somatic reactions. In this way, human beings come to be dominated by their physiological mechanisms.

Mistaken concept of virility

The ease with which it is possible to stimulate sexual excitement encourages many people to search for pleasure and the subsequent easing of tension. But this sort of excitement, above all when not determined by the will, is quite easily curbed by the will. For what differentiates us human beings from the animals is our ability to control our own reactions. The secretion of the gametes is independent of the human will; sexual activity, however, is always a result of the free decision of the individual. Often people not only say "I want" but also "I ought to do it," and this "I ought" is not a real physiological necessity, but only a reinforcing of "I want." But if the mere permissive attitude, "I want," is already enough to stimulate excitement, the prohibition, "I mustn't," is not enough to curb the reaction. And here lies the most difficult problem: prohibition is not only of little use but in many cases produces the opposite effect; by releasing the transgressive mechanisms, it increases the excitement. Boys who try to give up masturbating often make the mistake of repeating over and over to themselves the prohibition, "mustn't do it because it is a sin." Simple prohibition, therefore, is not the right approach, since it creates further tension and is hard to put into practice; what is important, though, is the conscious free choice: "I do not commit the sin, not because it is forbidden to do so but because I am conscious of the fact that it is wrong and give it up of my own free will."

Identical considerations hold true for priestly celibacy: if the candidate for the priesthood is not deeply motivated in making his choice and renouncing matrimony, he will never appreciate the value of chastity and totally immerse himself in God's love.

Celibacy as a life-style

In choosing a way of life, a man who is psychologically mature ought to be quite clear too about the way his decision will work out in practice and be aware of the results and of the responsibilities involved. Many factors contribute in differing degrees to psychological and emotional maturity, but above all the repeated and constant work one does on oneself. As complex entities, we have the task of realizing our capacities, but only by uninterrupted effort can we reach that degree of maturity which Karol Wojtyla calls "self-possession" (e.g., in *The Acting Person*, 1979), which is indispensable for the realizing of any vocation.

Priesthood precludes marriage not so much because the Church has decided that it does, but rather because, requiring an absolute devotion, it leaves no room for the commitment, equally total, demanded by marriage and fatherhood. Unfortunately, the future priest often lives in an environment where the hedonistic attitude prevails, and hence the ideal of total devotion is not respected.

Asceticism in the Christian's life

In today's world, believers often do not manage rationally to grasp the deeper sense of Christianity. Loving our neighbour involves a need for renunciation; helping the person loved sometimes requires a real sacrifice. Life in Christ demands a constant availability to sacrifice; all the more so, the life of someone proposing to enter Holy Orders.

Of the various values one is called upon to renounce in order to become a priest, there is also the possibility of exercising one's own sexuality. But because it is commonly thought that sexual activity is to be identified only with pleasure, the requirement of celibacy is seen as deprivation of that pleasure. From the point of view of the physiology of the human body, the renunciation of sexual activity does not mean the mortification of any one particular demand, since the body does not possess mechanisms constraining it to act in this way. The male genital organs, the constant activity of the gonads as endocrine glands notwithstanding, do not react without being stimulated. Chastity therefore does not exert any negative effect on the organism; indeed one might say there is a saving of energy, permitting the subject to concentrate his attention on other activities.

Now, to reach such a state of harmonious equilibrium, and beyond a decisive attitude of will, one needs to live an ordered life, maintaining a certain physical and psychic "hygiene" and inner discipline. It is also necessary to understand how one's body works, to know its reactions and the mechanisms that trigger them. By knowing the way one's body reacts, one can avoid the stimuli that provoke unwanted reactions, since our body is obedient to our will, if we learn how to control it. The somatic reactions are always conditioned by an external impulse; and, hence, as it is possible to make it more sensitive to external stimuli, so it is possible also to control it in such a way that it does not respond to such stimuli. The boy, as he matures, learns to understand the mechanism of his own reactions and how to control them.

In practice, we are all obliged to acquire this ability to control our own reactions, for the very demands of social life compel us to do so. The sexual act, belonging as it does to the most intimate sphere of our entity, never takes place spontaneously under the impulse of the moment, but always has to have a context and a right moment; and this involves the necessity of controlling the somatic reactions. Spontaneity, in the literal sense of the word, does not exist in human sexual activity.

Now, the priest, by virtue of the vocation he has chosen, has to be aware that for him the possibility of activating the mechanisms of sexual reaction does not exist and that, by activating them, he comes into collision with himself and the vow he has pronounced. From situations of this sort, neuroses can arise: it is not celibacy that creates the stress but the lack of firmness in carrying it out on account of psychical immaturity, simple human weakness, or insufficient acceptance of the ideal of celibacy itself.

On the other hand, if the candidate for the priesthood learns to avoid the stimuli and if he looks on other people as one big family, as Jesus teaches, he will not mind abstinence particularly, nor will he yearn for a different lifestyle, since the one he has chosen makes him happy and fulfilled.

MATURITY AND RELIGIOUS REALISM

In the process of maturing physically and mentally, we each become aware of the purpose of our own existence and of the meaning of life as such. For the believer, maturity means being aware of the limitations of earthly life, and the eternity of life in God. The prospect of eternity helps us patiently to endure the hardships that may turn up in life, thanks to our being aware that they are only fleeting. The priest's job is not only to point out the true dimension of human existence to believers, but also to bear witness to it in his own life. The words of Jesus on the Last Judgment have particular relevance for those individuals to whom "more has been given." The priest, by his nature, represents the apogee of human potentiality: no higher dignity exists, nor greater responsibility.

Now, awareness of responsibility, which God's gift entails, constrains us to reflect deeply. The gift of sexuality is not simply a gift but, like all life, is also a task laid before us. Chastity does not in fact constitute an absence of positive experience but, on the contrary, through the effort of the will, a means of reaching a state of equilibrium, an inexhaustible sense of satisfaction and joy. The sex act offers only a second of pleasure and often leaves a feeling of shame and embarrassment as regards one's own reactions. The knowledge of having full power over one's own instinctual reactions, however, gives one not only real joy but above all a feeling of freedom, since only at the time when we become capable of living in conformity to the chosen system of values can we say that we are truly free. The happiness that comes from this is pure and lasting, and it helps us to achieve a state of psychic equilibrium.

People who manage to realize these principles in daily life radiate their own inner peace and harmony to others. The influence that priests endowed with this particular ability exert on other people is enormous, since the need for peace is common to all. Sin always makes for anxiety; virtue, even if dearly purchased, brings joy. Besides awareness of the grace of which he is trustee, the privilege of offering God to others in the sacraments ought to fill the priest with still greater joy and gratitude for his vocation. In such a situation, celibacy cannot constitute a real hardship, since he is so filled with grace and divine love as to forget all about himself, as the lives of many a holy priest bear witness.

DIFFICULTIES IN OBSERVING CELIBACY

Today's way of thinking presents an obstacle to the ideal of priesthood as the quest for personal sanctity and the sanctification of the world. The difficulties the priest encounters in following his vocation are of various kinds, but those connected with the observance of celibacy are particularly grave, since transgressing this obligation usually means sinning against the sixth commandment. A religious, in point of fact, rarely asks for a dispensation and permission to get married before having committed the sin. But it cannot be forgotten that in the life of the priest there no longer exists a power of choosing between priesthood and marriage: the choice has already been taken and is to all intents and purposes irrevocable, for reneging on one's own commitment signifies moral degradation.

(a) *Mistaken concept of sexuality.* Difficulties are likely to arise once the priest gives in to the widely held view that human beings are biologically determined. The erroneous notion that the male is, in a sense, compelled to sexual activity by virtue of the very fact of being male is becoming ever more widespread. Many people even think that the sexual act "proves" a man's virility; that without it, a man is in some way disabled, unrealized. Concepts of this sort, especially if repeated by medical authorities in the sexological field (as often happens), can easily be used to justify one's own behavior. From now on, the individual, dominated by his own body, justifies himself by saying that "it is not possible" to act otherwise.

(b) The other factor that makes curbing one's sexuality more difficult is *physical and psychical exhaustion*, accompanied by an excess of stimuli, especially visual ones. People react particularly intensely to visual impressions, and Jesus Himself warns us against the temptations of the eye. If images of an erotic kind are added to stress, increased by the abuse of nicotine, caffeine, and the like, the mechanism of self-control may be weakened, especially in the young.

Chastity requires a constant discipline and a constant hygiene in one's life-style. By giving way to the stimulus, we cannot expect the body to be able to resist the somatic reactions easily; the body on its own does not have the ability to control its own reactions. Stimuli that may cause sexual reactions are of various kinds. The simplest sort— the mechanical ones, for instance—are generally easy to avoid, and even very young boys are usually able to curb them. More dangerous, however, are those which come from within us, from the imagination.

So it is extremely important for every priest to know how to maintain discipline over his thoughts and his imagination. For one can also sin alone, in thought: by looking at another person with desire, by treating that other person as an object, the sin of fornication is committed in the depths of the heart. If an attitude of this sort dominates the heart, it will also manifest itself outside. On the other hand, if we are clean within, no external situation can provoke somatic reactions against our will. Sexual excitement depends, in the first place, on the intentions with which we approach our neighbor, how we look at him or her, and what we see there. The priest is obliged to see the very Christ in his neighbor; the aim of any encounter can only be to bring that person nearer to God.

The entire human body shares in the specific vocation of each individual, for without a physical structure we cannot exist. So the body too has to help the priest in his task as the shepherd of souls. Maturity brings the father's role, particularly to the priest, whose task it is to beget souls (as Saint Paul expressed it).

Lust tends to subordinate others to our will, subjugating them and humiliating them by treating them as objects. A father's love, however, offers itself, asking nothing in return. But to attain to this, one must teach the body self-control. Chastity is, therefore, a constant effort to subject the body entirely to the aspirations of the soul. Each human being's body is always subject to a spirit: either to the Holy Spirit, or to "the spirit of this world."

(c) *The weight of the past.* Not without reason, in days gone by, did the Church demand virginity of candidates for the priesthood; for, one of the conditions making the observance of celibacy especially hard is the memory the body retains of its own past experiences. Return to God and renewal of the soul are always possible, but, since the body retains the memory of the past, even if the sin has been absolved, its effects persist. Being used to surrendering to a given type of reaction, the body finds it hard to submit to a new kind of discipline; as a result, those who have committed the sins of fornication or masturbation find the obligation of celibacy all the more difficult to observe. The same is true for pornographic pictures: the memory retained by the eye, if on the one hand it makes the whole sexual sector seem hateful, on the other hand it provokes excitement and internal conflict. Obviously the priest cannot be isolated from the world around him; the important thing is to protect that great gift of his chastity. Important to this end will be inner discipline, but more important still, the capacity for admiring the beauty radiated by innocence and chastity.

(d) *Lack of faith.* When we analyze the lives of those priests who have not managed to keep the obligation of celibacy, one cause stands out as common to almost all of them: moral degradation. Usually this sets in with a crisis of faith and a rejection of the rules laid down by the Church—that is to say, in the final analysis, with a lack of humility. Usually, the law of celibacy is broken by men who are too sure of themselves, who do not seek the support of divine love. Holiness, although it requires the individual's collaboration, is primarily the gift of divine grace, a gift that needs to be humbly asked for in prayer. When the passion for prayer grows cool, the priest more easily becomes a prey to the pressures of his environment.

Celibacy, as an attempt to overcome one's self and one's own frailty, is a going "against the current," is a challenge hurled at the world, but it is never a going against human nature. For, by the very fact of being human beings, we are able to control our own reactions, since we are not to be identified solely with our bodies: we are souls embodied, created by God and created in His likeness. The demand of celibacy does not exceed human capacities: Christ Himself shows us the way when He bids us to seek perfection.

The conscious quest for holiness is not against the individual, but against our individual paltriness, and it leads us to transcend ourselves. A full realization of priesthood and celibacy develops the human personality to its full potential and thus makes it easier to achieve the objective to which we all are summoned—holiness.

APPENDICES

On the Celibacy of the Priest

POPE PAUL VI

To the Bishops, Priests and Faithful of the Whole Catholic World.[1]

Priestly celibacy has been guarded by the Church for centuries as a brilliant jewel, and retains its value undiminished even in our time when the outlook of men and the state of the world have undergone such profound changes.

Amid the modern stirrings of opinion, a tendency has also been manifested, and even a desire expressed, to ask the Church to re-examine this characteristic institution. It is said that in the world of our time the observance of celibacy has come to be difficult or even impossible.

2. This state of affairs is troubling consciences, perplexing some priests and young aspirants to the priesthood; it is a cause for alarm in many of the faithful and constrains Us to fulfill the promise We made to the Council Fathers. We told them that it was Our intention to give new luster and strength to priestly celibacy in the world of today.[1] Since saying this We have, over a considerable period of time, earnestly implored the enlightenment and assistance of the Holy Spirit and have examined before God opinions and petitions which have come to Us from all over the world, notably from many pastors of God's Church.

3. The great question concerning the sacred celibacy of

Sacerdotalis Cælibatus, encyclical letter, June 24, 1967.

[1] Cf. Letter of October 10, 1965, to Cardinal Tisserant, read in the general session of the next day.

the clergy in the Church has long been before Our mind in its deep seriousness: Must that grave, ennobling obligation remain today for those who have the intention of receiving major orders? Is it possible and appropriate nowadays to observe such an obligation? Has the time not come to break the bond linking celibacy with the priesthood in the Church? Could the difficult observance of it not be made optional? Would this not be a way to help the priestly ministry and facilitate ecumenical approaches? And if the golden law of sacred celibacy is to remain, what reasons are there to show that it is holy and fitting? What means are to be taken to observe it, and how can it be changed from a burden to a help for the priestly life?

4. Our attention has rested particularly on the objections which have been and are still made in various forms against the retention of sacred celibacy. In virtue of Our apostolic office We are obliged by the importance, and indeed the complexity, of the subject to give faithful consideration to the facts and the problems they involve, at the same time bringing to them—as it is Our duty and Our mission to do—the light of truth which is Christ. Our intention is to do in all things the will of Him Who has called Us to this office and to show what we are in the Church: the servant of the servants of God.

5. It may be said that today ecclesiastical celibacy has been examined more penetratingly than ever before and in all its aspects. It has been examined from the doctrinal, historical, sociological, psychological and pastoral point of view. The intentions prompting this examination have frequently been basically correct although reports may sometimes have distorted them.

Let us look openly at the principal objections against the law that links ecclesiastical celibacy with the priesthood.

The first seems to come from the most authoritative source, the New Testament which preserves the teaching of Christ and the Apostles. It does not openly demand celibacy of sacred ministers but proposes it rather as a free act of obedience to a special vocation or to a special spiritual gift.[2] Jesus Himself did not make it a prerequisite in His choice of the Twelve, nor did the Apostles for those who presided over the first Christian communities.[3]

6. The close relationship that the Fathers of the Church and ecclesiastical writers established over the centuries between the ministering priesthood and celibacy has its origin partly in a mentality and partly in historical circumstances far different from ours. In patristic texts we more frequently find exhortations to the clergy to abstain from marital relations rather than to observe celibacy; and the reasons justifying the perfect chastity of the Church's ministers seem often to be based on an overly pessimistic view of man's earthly condition or on a certain notion of the purity necessary for contact with sacred things. In addition, it is said that the old arguments no longer are in harmony with the different social and cultural milieus in which the Church today, through her priests, is called upon to work.

7. Many see a difficulty in the fact that in the present discipline concerning celibacy the gift of a vocation to the priesthood is identified with that of perfect chastity as a state of life for God's ministers. And so, people ask whether it is right to exclude from the priesthood those who, it is claimed, have been called to the ministry without having been called to lead a celibate life.

8. It is asserted, moreover, that the maintaining of priestly celibacy in the Church does great harm in those

[2] Cf. Mt 19:11f.
[3] Cf. 1 Tm 3:2–5; Ti 1:5–6.

regions where the shortage of the clergy—a fact recognized with sadness and deplored by the same Council [4]—gives rise to critical situations: that it prevents the full realization of the divine plan of salvation and at times jeopardizes the very possibility of the initial proclamation of the Gospel. Thus the disquieting decline in the ranks of the clergy is attributed by some to the heavy burden of the obligation of celibacy.

9. Then there are those who are convinced that a married priesthood would remove the occasions for infidelity, waywardness and distressing defections which hurt and sadden the whole Church. These also maintain that a married priesthood would enable Christ's ministers to witness more fully to Christian living by including the witness of married life, from which they are excluded by their state of life.

10. There are also some who strongly maintain that priests by reason of their celibacy find themselves in a situation that is not only against nature but also physically and psychologically detrimental to the development of a mature and well-balanced human personality. And so it happens, they say, that priests often become hard and lacking in human warmth; that, excluded from sharing fully the life and destiny of the rest of their brothers, they are obliged to live a life of solitude which leads to bitterness and discouragement.

So they ask: Don't all these things indicate that celibacy does unwarranted violence to nature and unjustifiably disparages human values which have their source in the divine work of creation and have been made whole through the work of the Redemption accomplished by Christ?

---

[4] Cf. *Christus Dominus* [CD], no. 35; *Apostolicam Actuositatem*, no. 1; *Presbyterorum Ordinis* [PO], nos. 10ff; *Ad Gentes*, nos. 19, 38.

11. Again, in view of the way in which a candidate for the priesthood comes to accept an obligation as momentous as this, the objection is raised that in practice this acceptance results not from an authentically personal decision, but rather from an attitude of passivity, the fruit of a formation that neither is adequate nor makes sufficient allowance for human liberty. For the degree of knowledge and power of decision of a young person and his psychological and physical maturity fall far below—or at any rate are disproportionate to—the seriousness of the obligation he is assuming, its real difficulties and its permanence.

12. We well realize that there are other objections that can be made against priestly celibacy. This is a very complex question, which touches intimately upon the very meaning of being alive, yet is penetrated and resolved by the light of Divine Revelation. A never-ending series of difficulties will present themselves to those who cannot "receive this precept"[5] and who do not know or have forgotten it is a "gift of God,"[6] and who moreover are unaware of the loftier reasoning, wonderful efficacy and abundant riches of this new insight into life.

13. The sum of these objections would appear to drown out the solemn and age-old voice of the pastors of the Church and of the masters of the spiritual life, and to nullify the living testimony of the countless ranks of saints and faithful ministers of God, for whom celibacy has been the object of the total and generous gift of themselves to the mystery of Christ, as well as its outward sign. But no, this voice, still strong and untroubled, is the voice not just of the past but of the present too. Ever intent on the realities of today, we cannot close our eyes to this magnificent,

[5] Mt 19:11.
[6] Jn 4:10.

wonderful reality: that there are still today in God's holy Church, in every part of the world where she exercises her beneficent influence, great numbers of her ministers—subdeacons, deacons, priests and bishops—who are living their life of voluntary and consecrated celibacy in the most exemplary way.

Nor can we overlook the immense ranks of men and women in religious life, of laity and of young people too, united in the faithful observance of perfect chastity. They live in chastity, not out of disdain for the gift of life, but because of a greater love for that new life which springs from the Paschal Mystery. They live this life of courageous self-denial and spiritual joyfulness with exemplary fidelity and also with relative facility. This magnificent phenomenon bears testimony to an exceptional facet of the Kingdom of God living in the midst of modern society, to which it renders humble and beneficial service as the "light of the world" and the "salt of the earth."[7] We cannot withhold the expression of our admiration; the spirit of Christ is certainly breathing here.

14. Hence We consider that the present law of celibacy should today continue to be linked to the ecclesiastical ministry. This law should support the minister in his exclusive, definitive and total choice of the unique and supreme love of Christ; it should uphold him in the entire dedication of himself to the public worship of God and to the service of the Church; it should distinguish his state of life both among the faithful and in the world at large.

15. The gift of the priestly vocation dedicated to the divine worship and to the religious and pastoral service of the People of God, is undoubtedly distinct from that which

---

[7] Mt 5:13f.

leads a person to choose celibacy as a state of consecrated life.[8] But the priestly vocation, although inspired by God, does not become definitive or operative without having been tested and accepted by those in the Church who hold power and bear responsibility for the ministry serving the ecclesial community. It is, therefore, the task of those who hold authority in the Church to determine, in accordance with the varying conditions of time and place, who in actual practice are to be considered suitable candidates for the religious and pastoral service of the Church, and what should be required of them.

16. In a spirit of faith, therefore, We look on this occasion afforded Us by Divine Providence as a favorable opportunity for setting forth anew, and in a way more suited to the men of our time, the fundamental reasons for sacred celibacy. If difficulties against faith "can stimulate our minds to a more accurate and deeper understanding" of it,[9] the same is true of the ecclesiastical discipline which guides and directs the life of the faithful.

We are deeply moved by the joy this occasion gives Us of contemplating the richness in virtue and the beauty of the Church of Christ. These may not always be immediately apparent to the human eye, because they derive from the love of the divine Head of the Church and because they are revealed in the perfection of holiness [10] which moves the human spirit to admiration, and which human resources cannot adequately explain.

17. Virginity undoubtedly, as the Second Vatican Council declared, "is not, of course, required by the nature of the priesthood itself. This is clear from the practice of the early

[8] Cf. above, nos. 5, 7.
[9] *Gaudium et Spes* [GS], no. 62.
[10] Cf. Eph 5:25–27.

Church and the traditions of the Eastern Churches." [11] But at the same time the Council did not hesitate to confirm solemnly the ancient, sacred and providential present law of priestly celibacy. In addition, it set forth the motives which justify this law for those who, in a spirit of faith and with generous fervor, know how to appreciate the gifts of God.

18. Consideration of how celibacy is "particularly suited" [12] to God's ministers is not something recent. Even if the explicit reasons have differed with different mentalities and different situations, they were always inspired by specifically Christian considerations; and from these considerations we can get an intuition of the more fundamental motives underlying them. [13] These can be brought into clearer light only under the influence of the Holy Spirit, promised by Christ to His followers for the knowledge of things to come [14] and to enable the People of God to increase in the understanding of the mystery of Christ and of the Church. In this process the experience gained through the ages from a deeper penetration of spiritual things also has its part.

19. The Christian priesthood, being of a new order, can be understood only in the light of the newness of Christ, the Supreme Pontiff and eternal Priest, Who instituted the priesthood of the ministry as a real participation in His own unique priesthood. [15] The minister of Christ and dispenser of the mysteries of God, [16] therefore, looks up to

[11] PO, no. 16.
[12] Ibid.
[13] Cf. *Dei Verbum*, no. 8.
[14] Cf. Jn 16:13.
[15] Cf. *Lumen Gentium* [LG], no. 28; PO, no. 2.
[16] Cf. 1 Cor 4:1.

Him directly as his model and supreme ideal.[17] The Lord
Jesus, the only Son of God, was sent by the Father into the
world and He became Man, in order that humanity which
was subject to sin and death might be reborn, and through
this new birth[18] might enter the Kingdom of Heaven. Being
entirely consecrated to the will of the Father,[19] Jesus
brought forth this new creation by means of His Paschal
Mystery;[20] thus, He introduced into time and into the
world a new form of life which is sublime and divine and
which radically transforms the human condition.[21]

20. Matrimony, according to the will of God, continues
the work of the first creation;[22] and considered within the
total plan of salvation, it even acquired a new meaning and
a new value. Jesus, in fact, has restored its original dignity,[23]
has honored it[24] and has raised it to the dignity of a sacrament and of a mysterious symbol of His own union with
the Church.[25] Thus, Christian couples walk together toward their heavenly fatherland in the exercise of mutual
love, in the fulfillment of their particular obligations, and in
striving for the sanctity proper to them. But Christ, "Mediator of a superior covenant,"[26] has also opened a new
way, in which the human creature adheres wholly and directly to the Lord, and is concerned only with Him and
with His affairs;[27] thus, He manifests in a clearer and more

[17] Cf. 1 Cor 11:1.
[18] Cf. Jn 3:5; Ti 3:5.
[19] Cf. Jn 4:34; 17:4.
[20] Cf. 2 Cor 5:17; Gal 6:15.
[21] Cf. Gal 3:28.
[22] Cf. Gen 2:18.
[23] Cf. Mt 19:3–8.
[24] Cf. Jn 2:1–11.
[25] Cf. Eph 5:32.
[26] Heb 8:6.
[27] Cf. 1 Cor 7:33–35.

complete way the profoundly transforming reality of the New Testament.

21. Christ, the only Son of the Father, by the power of the Incarnation itself was made Mediator between heaven and earth, between the Father and the human race. Wholly in accord with this mission, Christ remained throughout His whole life in the state of celibacy, which signified His total dedication to the service of God and men. This deep connection between celibacy and the priesthood of Christ is reflected in those whose fortune it is to share in the dignity and mission of the Mediator and eternal Priest; this sharing will be more perfect the freer the sacred minister is from the bonds of flesh and blood.[28]

22. Jesus, Who selected the first ministers of salvation, wished them to be introduced to the understanding of the "mysteries of the kingdom of heaven,"[29] but He also wished them to be coworkers with God under a very special title, and His ambassadors.[30] He called them friends and brethren,[31] for whom He consecrated Himself so that they might be consecrated in truth;[32] He promised a more than abundant recompense to anyone who should leave home, family, wife and children for the sake of the Kingdom of God.[33] More than this, in words filled with mystery and hope, He also commended an even more perfect consecration[34] to the Kingdom of Heaven by means of celibacy, as a special gift.[35] The motive of this response to the divine

[28] Cf. PO, n.16.
[29] Cf. Mt 13:11; Mk 4:11; Lk 8:10.
[30] Cf. 2 Cor 5:20.
[31] Cf. Jn 15:15; 20:17.
[32] Cf. Jn 7:19.
[33] Cf. Lk 18:29–30.
[34] Cf. PO, no. 16.
[35] Cf. Mt 19:11.

call is the Kingdom of Heaven;[36] similarly, this very Kingdom,[37] the Gospel[38] and the name of Christ[39] motivate
those called by Jesus to undertake the work of the
apostolate, freely accepting its burdens, that they may participate the more closely in His lot.

23. To them this is the mystery of the newness of Christ,
of all that He is and stands for; it is the sum of the highest
ideals of the Gospel and of the Kingdom; it is a particular
manifestation of grace, which springs from the Paschal
Mystery of the Savior. This is what makes the choice of
celibacy desirable and worthwhile to those called by our
Lord Jesus. Thus they intend not only to participate in His
priestly office, but also to share with Him His very condition of living.

24. The response to the divine call is an answer of love
to the love which Christ has shown us so sublimely.[40] This
response is included in the mystery of that special love for
souls who have accepted His most urgent appeals.[41] With a
divine force, grace increases the longings of love. And
love, when it is genuine, is all-embracing, stable and lasting, an irresistible spur to all forms of heroism. And so the
free choice of sacred celibacy has always been considered
by the Church "as a symbol of, and stimulus to, charity":[42] It signifies a love without reservations; it stimulates
to a charity which is open to all. In a life so completely
dedicated and motivated, who can see the sign of spiritual
narrowness or self-seeking, and not see rather that celi-

---

[36] Cf. Mt 19:12.
[37] Cf. Lk 18:29f.
[38] Cf. Mk 10:29f.
[39] Cf. Mt 19:29.
[40] Cf. Jn 3:16; 15:13.
[41] Cf. Mk 10:21.
[42] LG, no. 42.

bacy is and ought to be a rare and very meaningful example of a life motivated by love, by which man expresses his own unique greatness? Who can doubt the moral and spiritual richness of such a life, consecrated not to any human ideal, no matter how noble, but to Christ and to His work to bring about a new form of humanity in all places and for all generations?

25. This biblical and theological view associates our ministerial priesthood with the priesthood of Christ; the total and exclusive dedication of Christ to His mission of salvation provides reason and example for our assimilation to the form of charity and sacrifice proper to Christ our Savior. This vision seems to Us so profound and rich in truth, both speculative and practical, that We invite you, venerable brothers, and you, eager students of Christian doctrine and masters of the spiritual life, and all you priests who have gained a supernatural insight into your vocation, to persevere in the study of this vision, and to go deeply into the inner recesses and wealth of its reality. In this way, the bond between the priesthood and celibacy will more and more be seen as closely knit as the mark of a heroic soul and the imperative call to unique and total love for Christ and His Church.

26. "Laid hold of by Christ"[43] unto the complete abandonment of one's entire self to Him, the priest takes on a closer likeness to Christ, even in the love with which the eternal Priest has loved the Church His Body and offered Himself entirely for her sake, in order to make her a glorious, holy and immaculate Spouse.[44]

The consecrated celibacy of the sacred ministers actually manifests the virginal love of Christ for the Church, and

[43] Phil 3:12.
[44] Cf. Eph 5:25–27.

the virginal and supernatural fecundity of this marriage, by which the children of God are born, "not of blood, nor of the will of the flesh." [45] [46]

27. The priest dedicates himself to the service of the Lord Jesus and of His Mystical Body with complete liberty, which is made easier by his total offering, and thus he depicts more fully the unity and harmony of the priestly life.[47] His ability for listening to the Word of God and for prayer increases. Indeed, the Word of God, as preserved by the Church, stirs up vibrant and profound echoes in the priest who daily meditates on it, lives it and preaches it to the faithful.

28. Like Christ Himself, His minister is wholly and solely intent on the things of God and the Church,[48] and he imitates the great High Priest Who lives ever in the presence of God in order to intercede in our favor.[49] So he receives joy and encouragement unceasingly from the attentive and devout recitation of the Divine Office, by which he dedicates his voice to the Church who prays together with her Spouse,[50] and he recognizes the necessity of continuing his diligence at prayer, which is the profoundly priestly occupation.[51]

29. The rest of a priest's life also acquires a greater richness of meaning and sanctifying power. In fact, his individual efforts at his own sanctification find new incentives in the ministry of grace and in the ministry of the Eucharist, in which "the whole spiritual good of the Church is

[45] Jn 1:13.
[46] Cf. LG, no. 42; PO, no. 16.
[47] Cf. PO, no. 14.
[48] Cf. Lk 2:49; 1 Cor 7:32f.
[49] Cf. Heb 9:24; 7:25.
[50] Cf. PO, no. 13.
[51] Cf. Acts 6:4.

contained": [52] acting in the Person of Christ, the priest unites himself most intimately with the offering, and places on the altar his entire life, which bears the marks of the holocaust.

30. What other considerations can We offer to describe the increase of the priest's power, his service, his love and sacrifice for the entire People of God? Christ spoke of Himself when He said: "Unless a grain of wheat falls into the earth and dies, it remains alone; but if it dies, it bears much fruit." [53] And the Apostle Paul did not hesitate to expose himself to a daily death in order to obtain among his faithful glory in Christ Jesus. [54] In a similar way, by a daily dying to himself and by giving up the legitimate love of a family of his own for the love of Christ and of His Kingdom, the priest will find the glory of an exceedingly rich and fruitful life in Christ, because like Him and in Him, he loves and dedicates himself to all the children of God.

31. In the community of the faithful committed to his charge, the priest represents Christ. Thus, it is most fitting that in all things he should reproduce the image of Christ and in particular follow His example, both in his personal and in his apostolic life. To his children in Christ, the priest is a sign and a pledge of that sublime and new reality which is the Kingdom of God; he dispenses it and he possesses it to a more perfect degree. Thus he nourishes the faith and hope of all Christians, who, as such, are bound to observe chastity according to their proper state of life.

32. The consecration to Christ under an additional and lofty title like celibacy evidently gives to the priest, even in

[52] PO, no. 5.
[53] Jn 12:24f.
[54] Cf. 1 Cor 15:31.

the practical field, the maximum efficiency and the best disposition of mind, mentally and emotionally, for the continuous exercise of a perfect charity.[55] This charity will permit him to spend himself wholly for the welfare of all, in a fuller and more concrete way.[56] It also obviously guarantees him a greater freedom and flexibility in the pastoral ministry,[57] in his active and living presence in the world, to which Christ has sent him,[58] so that he may pay fully to all the children of God the debt due to them.[59]

33. The Kingdom of God, which "is not of this world," [60] is present here on earth in mystery, and will reach its perfection only with the glorious coming of the Lord Jesus.[61] The Church here below constitutes the seed and the beginning of this Kingdom. And as she continues to grow slowly but surely, she longs for the perfect kingdom and ardently desires with all her energy to unite herself with her King in glory.[62] The pilgrim People of God are on a journey through the vicissitudes of this life toward their heavenly homeland,[63] where the divine sonship of the redeemed[64] will be fully revealed and where the transformed loveliness of the Spouse of the Lamb of God will shine completely.[65]

34. Our Lord and Master has said that "in the resurrection they neither marry nor are given in marriage, but are

[55] Cf. OT, no. 10.
[56] Cf. 2 Cor 12:15.
[57] Cf. PO, no. 16.
[58] Cf. Jn 17:18.
[59] Cf. Rom 1:14.
[60] Jn 18:36.
[61] Cf. GS, no. 39.
[62] Cf. LG, no. 5.
[63] Cf. Phil 3:20.
[64] Cf. 1 Jn 3:2.
[65] Cf. LG, no. 48.

like angels in heaven." [66] In the world of man, so deeply involved in earthly concerns and too often enslaved by the desires of the flesh,[67] the precious and almost divine gift of perfect continence for the Kingdom of Heaven stands out precisely as "a special token of the rewards of heaven"; [68] it proclaims the presence on earth of the final stages of salvation [69] with the arrival of a new world, and in a way it anticipates the fulfillment of the Kingdom as it sets forth its supreme values which will one day shine forth in all the children of God. This continence, therefore, stands as a testimony to the ever continuing progress of the People of God toward the final goal of their earthly pilgrimage, and as a stimulus for all to raise their eyes to the things above, "where Christ is seated at the right hand of God" and where "our life is hid with Christ in God" until it appears "with him in glory." [70]

35. Although it would be highly instructive to go through the writings of past centuries on ecclesiastical celibacy, this would take so long that We will let a brief account suffice. In Christian antiquity the Fathers and ecclesiastical writers testify to the spread through the East and the West of the voluntary practice of celibacy by sacred

[66] Mt 22:30.
[67] Cf. 1 Jn 2:16.
[68] PC, no. 12.
[69] Cf. 1 Cor 7:29–31.
[70] Col 3:1–4.
[71] Cf. Tertullian, De exhort. castitatis, 13: PL 2:930; St. Epiphanius, Adv. Hær. II, 48.9 and 59.4: PG 41:869, 1025; St. Ephrem, Carmina nisibena, XVIII, XIX: ed. G. Bickell, Leipzig (1866), p. 122; Eusebius of Cæsarea, Demonstr. evan., 1.9: PG 22:81; St. Cyril of Jerusalem, Catechesis, 12.25: PG 33:757; St. Ambrose, De officiis ministr., 1.50: PL 16:97ff.; St. Augustine, De moribus Eccl. cath., 1.32: PL 32:1339; St. Jerome, Adversus Vigilantium, 2: PL 23:34041; Bishop Synesius of Ptolemais, Epist. 105: PG 66:1485.

ministers[71] because of its profound suitability for their total dedication to the service of Christ and His Church.

36. From the beginning of the fourth century, the Church of the West strengthened, spread and confirmed this practice by means of various provincial councils and through the supreme pontiffs.[72] More than anyone else, the supreme pastors and teachers of the Church of God, the guardians and interpreters of the patrimony of the faith and of holy Christian practices, promoted, defended, and restored ecclesiastical celibacy in successive eras of history, even when they met opposition from the clergy itself and when the practices of a decadent society did not favor the heroic demands of virtue. The obligation of celibacy was then solemnly sanctioned by the Sacred Ecumenical Council of Trent[73] and finally included in the Code of Canon Law.[74]

37. The most recent sovereign pontiffs who preceded Us, making use of their doctrinal knowledge and spurred on by ardent zeal, strove to enlighten the clergy on this matter and to urge them to its observance.[75] We do not wish to fail to pay homage to them, especially to Our well-loved immediate predecessor, whose memory is still fresh in the hearts of men all over the world. During the Roman Synod, with the sincere approval of all the clergy of the city, he

[72] First done at the Council of Elvira, c. 300, canon 33: Mansi II, 11.

[73] Cf. Session XXIV, cc. 9–10

[74] Cf. canon 132, 1 [of the 1917 Code of Canon Law].

[75] Cf. St. Pius X, apost. exhortation *Hærent Animo*: AAS 41 (1908), 555–57; Benedict XV, letter to Francis Kordac, Archbishop of Prague: AAS 12 (1920), 57f; consistorial address, 16 December 1920: AAS 12 (1920), 585–88; Pius XI, encyc. letter *Ad Catholici Sacerdotii*: AAS 28 (1936), 24–30; Pius XII, apost. exhortation *Menti Nostræ*: AAS 42 (1950), 657–702; encyc. letter *Sacra Virginitas*: AAS 46 (1954), 161–91; John XXIII, encyc. letter *Sacerdotii Nostri Primordia*: AAS 51 (1959), 554–56.

spoke as follows: "It deeply hurts Us that . . . anyone can dream that the Church will deliberately or even suitably renounce what from time immemorial has been, and still remains, one of the purest and noblest glories of her priesthood. The law of ecclesiastical celibacy and the efforts necessary to preserve it always recall to mind the struggles of the heroic times when the Church of Christ had to fight for and succeeded in obtaining her threefold glory, always an emblem of victory, that is, the Church of Christ, free, chaste and catholic." [76]

38. If the legislation of the Eastern Church is different in the matter of discipline with regard to clerical celibacy, as was finally established by the Council of Trullo held in the year 692,[77] and which has been clearly recognized by the Second Vatican Council,[78] this is due to the different historical background of that most noble part of the Church, a situation which the Holy Spirit has providentially and supernaturally influenced.

We Ourselves take this opportunity to express Our esteem and Our respect for all the clergy of the Eastern Churches, and to recognize in them examples of fidelity and zeal which make them worthy of sincere veneration.

39. We find further comforting reasons for continuing to adhere to the observance of the discipline of clerical celibacy in the exaltation of virginity by the Eastern Fathers. We hear within Us, for example, the voice of St. Gregory of Nyssa, reminding us that "the life of virginity is the image of the blessedness that awaits us in the life to come." [79] We are no less assured by St. John Chrysostom's

[76] Second address, 26 January 1960: AAS 52 (1960), 226.
[77] Cf. Cc. 6, 12, 13, 48: Mansi 9:944–48, 965.
[78] Cf. PO, no. 16.
[79] De Virginitate, 13: PG [vol number?]:81–82.

treatise on the priesthood, which is still a fruitful subject for reflection. Intent on throwing light on the harmony which must exist between the private life of him who ministers at the altar and the dignity of the order to which his sacred duties belong, he affirmed: ". . . it is becoming that he who accepts the priesthood be as pure as if he were in heaven." [80]

40. Further, it is by no means futile to observe that in the East only celibate priests are ordained bishops, and priests themselves cannot contract marriage after their ordination to the priesthood. This indicates that these venerable Churches also possess to a certain extent the principle of a celibate priesthood and even of the appropriateness of celibacy for the Christian priesthood, of which the bishops possess the summit and fullness. [81]

41. In any case, the Church of the West cannot weaken her faithful observance of her own tradition. Nor can she be regarded as having followed for centuries a path which instead of favoring the spiritual richness of individual souls and of the People of God, has in some way compromised it, or of having stifled, with arbitrary juridical prescriptions, the free expansion of the most profound realities of nature and of grace.

42. In virtue of the fundamental norm of the government of the Catholic Church, to which We alluded above, [82] while on the one hand, the law requiring a freely chosen and perpetual celibacy of those who are admitted to Holy Orders remains unchanged, on the other hand, a study may be allowed of the particular circumstances of married sacred ministers of Churches or other Christian communities

[80] *De Sacerdotio*, I, III: PG 48:642.
[81] Cf. LG, nos. 21, 28, 64.
[82] Cf. above, no. 15.

separated from the Catholic communion, and of the possibility of admitting to priestly functions those who desire to adhere to the fullness of this communion and to continue to exercise the sacred ministry. The circumstances must be such, however, as not to prejudice the existing discipline regarding celibacy.

And that the authority of the Church does not hesitate to exercise her power in this matter can be seen from the recent Ecumenical Council, which foresaw the possibility of conferring the holy diaconate on men of mature age who are already married.[83]

43. All this, however, does not signify a relaxation of the existing law, and must not be interpreted as a prelude to its abolition. There are better things to do than to promote this hypothesis, which tears down that vigor and love in which celibacy finds security and happiness, and which obscures the true doctrine that justifies its existence and exalts its splendor. It would be much better to promote serious studies in defense of the spiritual meaning and moral value of virginity and celibacy.[84]

44. Holy virginity is a very special gift. Nevertheless, the whole present–day Church, solemnly and universally represented by the pastors responsible for her welfare (with due respect, as We have said, for the discipline of the Eastern Churches), manifested her absolute faith "in the Holy Spirit that the grace of leading a celibate life, so desirable in the priesthood of the New Testament, will be readily granted by God the Father if those who by ordination share the priesthood of Christ humbly and earnestly ask it together with the whole Church." [85]

[83] Cf. LG, no. 29.
[84] Ibid., no. 42.
[85] PO, no. 16.

45. We wholeheartedly call on the entire People of God to do their duty in bringing about an increase in priestly vocations.[86] We ask them fervently to beg the Father of all, the divine Spouse of the Church, and the Holy Spirit, her principle of life, through the intercession of the Blessed Virgin Mary, Mother of Christ and of His Church, to pour out, especially at present, this divine gift, which the Father certainly does not wish to give stingingly. They should also fervently pray, in like manner, that souls may dispose themselves to receive this gift by a profound faith and a generous love. In this way, in our world which needs God's glory,[87] priests, ever more perfectly conformed to the one and supreme Priest, will be a real glory to Christ,[88] and, through them, "the glory of the grace" of God will be magnified in the world of today.[89]

46. Yes, venerable and well-beloved brothers in the priesthood, whom We cherish "with the affection of Christ Jesus," [90] it is indeed this world in which we live, tormented by the pains of growth and change, justly proud of its human values and human conquests, which urgently needs the witness of lives consecrated to the highest and most sacred spiritual values. This witness is necessary in order that the rare and incomparable light radiating from the most sublime virtues of the spirit may not be wanting to our times.

47. Our Lord Jesus Christ did not hesitate to confide the formidable task of evangelizing the then-known world to a handful of men to all appearances lacking in number

[86] Cf. OT, no. 2; PO, no. 11.
[87] Cf. Rom 3:23.
[88] Cf. 2 Cor 8:23.
[89] Cf. Eph 1:6.
[90] Phil 1:8.

and quality. He bade this little flock not to lose heart,[91] for, thanks to His constant assistance,[92] through Him and with Him, they would overcome the world.[93] Jesus has also taught us that the Kingdom of God has an intrinsic and unobservable dynamism which enables it to grow "without [man's] knowing it."[94] The harvest of God's Kingdom is great, but the laborers, as in the beginning, are few. Actually, they have never been as numerous as human standards would have judged sufficient. But the heavenly King demands that we pray "the Lord of the harvest to send out laborers into His harvest."[95] The counsels and prudence of man cannot supersede the hidden wisdom of Him Who, in the history of salvation, has challenged man's wisdom and power by His own foolishness and weakness.[96]

48. Supported by the power of faith, We express the Church's conviction on this matter. Of this she is certain: If she is prompter and more persevering in her response to grace, if she relies more openly and more fully on its secret but invincible power, if, in short, she bears more exemplary witness to the mystery of Christ, then she will never fall short in the performance of her salvific mission to the world—no matter how much opposition she faces from human ways of thinking or misrepresentations. We must all realize that we can do all things in Him Who alone gives strength to souls[97] and increase to His Church.[98]

49. We are not easily led to believe that the abolition of

[91] Cf. Lk.12:32.
[92] Cf. Mt 28:20.
[93] Cf. Jn 16:33.
[94] Mk 4:26–29.
[95] Mt 9:37f.
[96] Cf. 1 Cor 1:20–31.
[97] Cf. Phil 4:13.
[98] Cf. 1 Cor 3:67.

ecclesiastical celibacy would considerably increase the number of priestly vocations: The contemporary experience of those Churches and ecclesial communities which allow their ministers to marry seems to prove the contrary. The causes of the decrease in vocations to the priesthood are to be found elsewhere—for example, in the fact that individuals and families have lost their sense of God and of all that is holy, their esteem for the Church as the institution of salvation through faith and the sacraments. The problem must be examined at its real source.

50. As We said above,[99] the Church is not unaware that the choice of consecrated celibacy, since it involves a series of hard renunciations which affect the very depths of a man, presents also grave difficulties and problems to which the men of today are particularly sensitive. In fact, it might seem that celibacy conflicts with the solemn recognition of human values by the Church in the recent Council. And yet more careful consideration reveals that this sacrifice of the human love experienced by most men in family life and given up by the priest for the love of Christ, is really a singular tribute paid to that great love. For it is universally recognized that man has always offered to God that which is worthy of both the giver and the receiver.

51. Moreover, the Church cannot and should not fail to realize that the choice of celibacy—provided that it is made with human and Christian prudence and responsibility—is governed by grace which, far from destroying or doing violence to nature, elevates it and imparts to it supernatural powers and vigor. God, Who has created and redeemed man, knows what He can ask of him and gives him everything necessary to be able to do what his Creator and

[99] Cf. above, no. 10.

147

Redeemer asks of him. St. Augustine, who had fully and painfully experienced in himself the nature of man, exclaimed: "Grant what You command, and command what You will." [100]

52. A true knowledge of the real difficulties of celibacy is very useful, even necessary, for the priest, so that he may be fully aware of what his celibacy requires in order to be genuine and beneficial. But with equal fidelity to the truth, these difficulties must not be given greater value or weight than they actually have in the human or religious sphere, or be declared impossible of solution.

53. Considering what contemporary scholarly investigation has ascertained, it is not right to continue repeating [101] that celibacy is against nature because it runs counter to lawful physical, psychic and affective needs, or to claim that a completely mature human personality demands fulfillment of these needs. Man, created to God's image and likeness, [102] is not just flesh and blood; the sexual instinct is not all that he has; man has also, and preeminently, understanding, choice, freedom, and thanks to these powers he is, and must remain, the chief work of creation; they give him mastery over his physical, mental and emotional appetites.

54. The true, profound reason for dedicated celibacy is, as We have said, the choice of a closer and more complete relationship with the mystery of Christ and the Church for the good of all mankind: In this choice there is no doubt that those highest human values are able to find their fullest expression.

55. The choice of celibacy does not connote ignorance

[100] *Conf.* X, 29, 40: PL 32:796.
[101] Cf. above, no. 10.
[102] Cf. Gen 1:26–27.

of or contempt for the sexual instinct and man's capacity for giving himself in love. That would certainly do damage to his physical and psychological balance. On the contrary, it demands clear understanding, careful self-control and a wise elevation of the mind to higher realities. In this way celibacy sets the whole man on a higher level and makes an effective contribution to his perfection.

56. We readily grant that the natural and lawful desire a man has to love a woman and to raise a family is renounced by the celibate in Sacred Orders; but it cannot be said that marriage and the family are the only way for fully developing the human person. In the priest's heart love is by no means extinct. His charity is drawn from the purest source,[103]practiced in the imitation of God and Christ, and is no less demanding and real than any other genuine love.[104] It gives the priest a limitless horizon, deepens and gives breadth to his sense of responsibility—a mark of mature personality—and inculcates in him, as a sign of a higher and greater fatherhood, a generosity and refinement of heart[105] which offer a superlative enrichment.

57. All the People of God must give testimony to the mystery of Christ and His Kingdom, but this witnessing does not take the same form for all. The Church leaves to her married children the function of giving the necessary testimony of a genuinely and fully Christian married and family life. She entrusts to her priests the testimony of a life wholly dedicated to pondering and seeking the new and delightful realities of God's Kingdom.

If this means that the priest is without a direct personal experience of married life, he nevertheless will be able through his training, his ministry and the grace of his

---

[103] Cf. 1 Jn 4:8–16.
[104] Cf. 1 Jn 3:16–18.

office, to gain even deeper insights into every human yearning. This will allow him to meet problems of this kind at their source and give solid support by his advice and assistance to married persons and Christian families.[106] For the Christian family, the example of the priest who is living his life of celibacy to the full will underscore the spiritual dimension of every love worthy of the name, and his personal sacrifice will merit for the faithful united in the holy bond of Matrimony the grace of a true union.

58. By reason of his celibacy, the priest is a man alone; that is true, but his solitude is not meaningless emptiness because it is filled with God and the brimming riches of His Kingdom. Moreover, he has prepared himself for this solitude—which should be an internal and external plenitude of charity—if he has chosen it with full understanding, and not through any proud desire to be different from the rest of men, or to withdraw himself from common responsibilities, or to alienate himself from his brothers, or to show contempt for the world. Though set apart from the world, the priest is not separated from the People of God, because he has been "appointed to act on behalf of men," [107] since he is "consecrated" completely to charity [108] and to the work for which the Lord has chosen him.[109]

59. At times loneliness will weigh heavily on the priest, but he will not for that reason regret having generously chosen it. Christ, too, in the most tragic hours of His life was alone—abandoned by the very ones whom He had chosen as witnesses to, and companions of, His life, and

---

[105] Cf. 1 Thes 2:11; 1 Cor 4:15; 1 Cor 6:13; Gal 4:19; 1 Tm 5:1–2.
[106] Cf. 1 Cor 2:15.
[107] Heb 5:1.
[108] Cf. 1 Cor 14:4ff.
[109] Cf. PO, no. 3.

whom He had loved "to the end" [110]—but He stated, "I am not alone, for the Father is with me." [111] He who has chosen to belong completely to Christ will find, above all, in intimacy with Him and in His grace, the power of spirit necessary to banish sadness and regret and to triumph over discouragement. He will not be lacking the protection of the Virgin Mother of Jesus nor the motherly solicitude of the Church, to whom he has given himself in service. He will not be without the kindly care of his father in Christ, his bishop; nor will the fraternal companionship of his fellow priests and the love of the entire People of God, most fruitful of consolations, be lacking to him. And if hostility, lack of confidence and the indifference of his fellow men make his solitude quite painful, he will thus be able to share, with dramatic clarity, the very experience of Christ, as an apostle who must not be "greater than he who sent him," [112] as a friend admitted to the most painful and most glorious secret of his divine Friend Who has chosen him to bring forth the mysterious fruit of life in his own life, which is only apparently one of death. [113]

60. Our reflection on the beauty, importance and intimate fittingness of holy virginity for the ministers of Christ and His Church makes it incumbent on those who hold the office of teacher and pastor of that Church to take steps to assure and promote its positive observance, from the first moment of preparation to receive such a precious gift.

In fact, the difficulties and problems which make the observance of chastity very painful or quite impossible for some, spring, not infrequently, from a type of priestly

[110] Jn 13:1.
[111] Jn 16:32.
[112] Jn 13:16; 15:18.
[113] Cf. Jn 15:15f, 20.

formation which, given the great changes of these last years, is no longer completely adequate for the formation of a personality worthy of a "man of God." [114]

61. The Second Vatican Council has already indicated wise criteria and guidelines to this end. They are in conformity with the progress of psychology and pedagogy, as well as with the changed conditions of mankind and of contemporary society.[115] It is Our wish that appropriate instructions be drawn up with the help of truly qualified men, treating with all necessary detail the theme of chastity. They should be sent out as soon as possible to provide competent and timely assistance to those who have the great responsibility within the Church of preparing future priests.

62. The priesthood is a ministry instituted by Christ for the service of His Mystical Body which is the Church. To her belongs the authority to admit to that priesthood those whom she judges qualified—that is, those to whom God has given, along with other signs of an ecclesiastical vocation, the gift of a consecrated celibacy.[116]

In virtue of such a gift, confirmed by canon law, the individual is called to respond with free judgment and total dedication, adapting his own mind and outlook to the will of God Who calls him. Concretely, this divine calling manifests itself in a given individual with his own definite personality structure which is not at all overpowered by grace. In candidates for the priesthood, therefore, the sense of receiving this divine gift should be cultivated; so too, a sense of responsibility in their meeting with God, with the highest importance given to supernatural means.

[114] 1 Tm 6:11.
[115] Cf. OT, nos. 3–11; PC, no. 12.
[116] Cf. above, no. 15.

63. It is likewise necessary that exact account be taken of the physical and psychological state of the candidate in order to guide and orient him toward the priestly ideal; so a truly adequate formation should harmoniously coordinate grace and nature in the man in whom one clearly sees the proper conditions and qualifications. These conditions should be ascertained as soon as signs of his holy vocation are first indicated—not hastily or superficially, but carefully, with the assistance and aid of a doctor or a competent psychologist. A serious investigation of hereditary factors should not be omitted.

64. Those who are discovered to be unfit for physical, psychological or moral reasons should be quickly removed from the path to the priesthood. Let educators appreciate that this is one of their very grave duties. They must neither indulge in false hopes and dangerous illusions nor permit the candidate to nourish these hopes in any way, with resultant damage to himself or to the Church. The life of the celibate priest, which engages the whole man so totally and so delicately, excludes in fact those of insufficient physical, psychic and moral qualifications. Nor should anyone pretend that grace supplies for the defects of nature in such a man.

65. After the capability of a man has been ascertained and he has been admitted to the course of studies leading to the goal of the priesthood, care should be taken for the progressive development of a mature personality through physical, intellectual and moral education directed toward the control and personal dominion of his temperament, sentiments and passions.

66. This will be proved by the firmness of the spirit with which he accepts the personal and community type of discipline demanded by the priestly life. Such a regime, the

lack or deficiency of which is to be deplored because it exposes the candidate to grave disorders, should not be borne only as an imposition from without. It should be inculcated and implanted as an indispensable component within the context of the spiritual life.

67. The educator should skillfully stimulate the young man to the evangelical virtue of sincerity [117] and to spontaneity by approving every good personal initiative, so that the young man will come to know and properly evaluate himself, wisely assume his own responsibilities, and train himself to that self-control which is of such importance in priestly education.

68. The exercise of authority, the principle of which should be maintained firmly, will be animated by wise moderation and a pastoral attitude. It will be used in a climate of dialogue and will be implemented in a gradual way which will afford the educator an ever-deepening understanding of the psychology of the young man, and will appeal to personal conviction.

69. The complete education of the candidate for the priesthood should be directed to help him acquire a tranquil, convinced and free choice of the grave responsibilities which he must assume in conscience before God and the Church. Ardor and generosity are marvelous qualities of youth; illuminated and supported, they merit, along with the blessing of the Lord, the admiration and confidence of the whole Church as well as of all men. None of the real personal and social difficulties which their choice will bring in its train should remain hidden to the young men, so that their enthusiasm will not be superficial and illusory. At the same time it will be right to highlight with at least equal

[117] Cf. Mt 5:37.

truth and clarity the sublimity of their choice, which, though it may lead on the one hand to a certain physical and psychic void, nevertheless on the other brings with it an interior richness capable of elevating the person most profoundly.

70. Young candidates for the priesthood should be convinced that they cannot follow their difficult way without a special type of asceticism proper to themselves and more demanding than that which is required of the other faithful. It will be a demanding asceticism but not a suffocating one which consists in the deliberate and assiduous practice of those virtues which make a man a priest: self-denial in the highest degree—an essential condition if one would follow Christ;[118] humility and obedience as expressions of internal truth and of an ordered liberty; prudence, justice, courage and temperance—virtues without which it is impossible for true and profound religious life to exist; a sense of responsibility, fidelity and loyalty in the acceptance of one's obligations; a balance between contemplation and action; detachment and a spirit of poverty, which will give tone and vigor to evangelical freedom; chastity, the result of a persevering struggle, harmonized with all the other natural and supernatural virtues; a serene and secure contact with the world to whose service the young man will dedicate himself for Christ and for His Kingdom.

In such a way the aspirant to the priesthood will acquire, with the help of a divine grace, a strong, mature and balanced personality, a combination of inherited and acquired qualities, harmony of all his powers in the light of the faith and in intimate union with Christ whom He has chosen for Himself and for the ministry of salvation to the world.

[118] Cf. Mt 16:24; Jn 12:25.

71. However, to judge with more certainty the young man's fitness for the priesthood and to have successive proofs of his attained maturity on both the human and supernatural levels—for "it is more difficult to conduct oneself correctly in the service of souls because of dangers coming from outside" [119]—it will be advisable to have a preliminary trial period before the observance of holy celibacy becomes something definitive and permanent through ordination to the priesthood. [120]

72. Once moral certainty has been obtained that the maturity of the candidate is sufficiently guaranteed, he will be in a position to take on himself the heavy and sweet burden of priestly chastity as a total gift of himself to the Lord and to His Church.

In this way, the obligation of celibacy, which the Church makes a condition of Holy Orders, is accepted by the candidate through the influence of divine grace and with full reflection and liberty, and, as is evident, not without the wise and prudent advice of competent spiritual directors who are concerned not to impose the choice, but rather to dispose the candidate to make it more consciously. Hence, in that solemn moment when the candidate will decide once and for his whole life, he will not feel the weight of an imposition from outside, but rather the interior joy that accompanies a choice made for the love of Christ.

73. The priest must not think that ordination makes everything easy for him and screens him once and for all from every temptation or danger. Chastity is not acquired all at once but results from a laborious conquest and daily affirmation. Our world today stresses the positive values of

[119] St. Thomas Aquinas, *Summa Theol.*, II-II, q. 184, a. 8 c.
[120] Cf. OT, no. 12.

love between the sexes but has also multiplied the difficulties and risks in this sphere. In order to safeguard his chastity with all care and affirm its sublime meaning, the priest must consider clearly and calmly his position as a man exposed to spiritual warfare against seductions of the flesh in himself and in the world, continually renewing his resolution to give an ever–increasing and ever better perfection to the irrevocable offering of himself which obliges him to a fidelity that is complete, loyal and real.

74. Christ's priest will daily receive new strength and joy as he deepens in meditation and prayer the motives for his gift and the conviction that he has chosen the better part. He will ask humbly and perseveringly for the grace of fidelity, never denied to those who ask it sincerely. At the same time he will use the natural and supernatural means at his disposal. In particular he will not disregard those ascetical norms which have been substantiated by the Church's experience and are no less necessary in modern circumstances than in former times.[121]

75. The priest should apply himself above all else to developing, with all the love grace inspires in him, his close relationship with Christ, and exploring this inexhaustible and enriching mystery; he should also acquire an ever deeper sense of the mystery of the Church. There would be the risk of his state of life seeming unreasonable and unfounded if it is viewed apart from this mystery.

Priestly piety, nourished at the table of God's Word and the Holy Eucharist, lived within the cycle of the liturgical year, inspired by a warm and enlightened devotion to the Virgin Mother of the supreme and eternal High Priest and Queen of the Apostles,[122] will bring him to the source of a

[121] Cf. PO, nos. 16, 18.
[122] Cf. ibid., no. 18.

true spiritual life which alone provides a solid foundation for the observance of celibacy.

76. In this way the priest, with grace and peace in his heart, will face with generosity the manifold tasks of his life and ministry. If he performs these with faith and zeal he will find in them new occasions to show that he belongs entirely to Christ and His Mystical Body, for his own sanctification and the sanctification of others. The charity of Christ which urges him on,[123] will help him not to renounce his higher feelings but to elevate and deepen them in a spirit of consecration in imitation of Christ the High Priest, Who shared intimately in the life of men, loved and suffered for them,[124] and of Paul the Apostle who shared in the cares of all,[125] in order to bring the light and power of the Gospel of God's grace to shine in the world.[126]

77. Rightly jealous of his full self-giving to the Lord, the priest should know how to guard against emotional tendencies which give rise to desires not sufficiently enlightened or guided by the Spirit. He should beware of seeing spiritual or apostolic pretexts for what are in fact dangerous inclinations of the heart.

78. The priestly life certainly requires an authentic spiritual intensity in order to live by the Spirit;[127] it requires a truly virile asceticism—both interior and exterior—in one who, belonging in a special way to Christ, has in Him and through Him "crucified the flesh with its passions and desires,"[128] not hesitating to face arduous and lengthy trials

---

[123] Cf. 2 Cor 5:14.
[124] Cf. Heb 4:15.
[125] Cf. 1 Cor 9:22; 2 Cor 11:29.
[126] Cf. Acts 20:24.
[127] Cf. Gal 5:25.
[128] Gal 5:24.

in order to do so.[129] In this way Christ's minister will be the better able to show to the world the fruits of the Spirit, which are "charity, joy, peace, patience, benignity, goodness, longanimity, mildness, faith, modesty. continency, chastity."[130]

79. Moreover, priestly chastity is increased, guarded and defended by a way of life, surroundings and activity suited to a minister of God. For this reason the "close sacramental brotherhood"[131] which all priests enjoy in virtue of their ordination must be fostered to the utmost. Our Lord Jesus Christ has taught the urgency of the new commandment of charity. He gave a wonderful example of it when He instituted the Sacrament of the Eucharist and the Catholic priesthood,[132] and prayed to His Heavenly Father that the love the Father bore for Him from all eternity should be in His ministers and that He too should be in them.[133]

80. So the unity of spirit among priests should be active in their prayers, friendship and help of all kinds for one another. One cannot sufficiently recommend to priests a life lived in common and directed entirely toward their sacred ministry; the practice of having frequent meetings with a fraternal exchange of ideas, counsel and experience with their brother priests; the movement to form associations which encourage priestly holiness.

81. Priests should reflect on the advice of the Council,[134] which reminds them of their common sharing in the priesthood so that they may feel a lively responsibility for fellow

---

[129] Cf. 1 Cor 9:26–27.
[130] Gal 5:22–23.
[131] Cf. PO, no. 8.
[132] Cf. Jn 13:15 and 34–35.
[133] Cf. Jn 17:26.
[134] Cf. PO, no. 8.

priests troubled by difficulties which gravely endanger the divine gift they have. They should have a burning charity for those who have greater need of love, understanding and prayer, who have need of prudent but effective help, and who have a claim on their unbounded charity as those who are, and should be, their truest friends.

82. Venerable brothers in the episcopacy, priests and ministers of the altar, by way of completing and leaving a remembrance of this written conversation with you, we should like to suggest this resolution to you: That on the anniversary of his ordination, or on Holy Thursday when all are united in spirit commemorating the mystery of the institution of the priesthood, each one should renew his total gift of himself to Christ our Lord; reviving in this way the awareness that He has chosen you for His divine service, and repeating at the same time, humbly and courageously, the promise of our unswerving faithfulness to His love alone in your offering of perfect chastity.[135]

83. Now, with fatherly love and affection, Our heart turns anxiously and with deep sorrow to those unfortunate priests who always remain Our dearly beloved brothers and whose absence We keenly regret. We speak of those who, retaining the sacred character conferred by their priestly ordination, have nonetheless been sadly unfaithful to the obligations they accepted when ordained.

Their sad state and its consequences to priests and to others move some to wonder if celibacy is not in some way responsible for such dramatic occurrences and for the scandals they inflict on God's People. In fact, the responsibility falls not on consecrated celibacy in itself but on a judgment of the fitness of the candidate of the priesthood which was

[135] Cf. Rom 12:1.

not always adequate or prudent at the proper time, or else it falls on the way in which sacred ministers live their life of total consecration.

84. The Church is very conscious of the sad state of these sons of hers and judges it necessary to make every effort to avert or to remedy the wounds she suffers by their defection. Following the example of Our immediate predecessors, We also have, in cases concerning ordination to the priesthood, been prepared to allow inquiry to extend beyond the provisions of the present canon law[136] to other very grave reasons which give ground for really solid doubts regarding the full freedom and responsibility of the candidate for the priesthood and his fitness for the priestly state. This has been done to free those who, on careful judicial consideration of their case, are seen to be really unsuited.

85. The dispensations which are granted after such considerations—minimal percentage when they are compared with the great number of good, worthy priests—provide in justice for the spiritual salvation of the individual and show at the same time the Church's concern to safeguard celibacy and the complete fidelity of all her ministers. In granting such dispensations the Church always acts with heartfelt regret, especially in the particularly lamentable cases in which refusal to bear worthily this sweet yoke of Christ results from crises in faith, or moral weakness, and is thus frequently a failure in responsibility and a source of scandal to the Christian people.

86. If these priests knew how much sorrow, dishonor and unrest they bring to the holy Church of God, if they reflected on the seriousness and beauty of their obligations

---

[136] Cf. *Code of Canon Law*, c. 214 [of the 1917 Code].

and on the dangers to which they are exposed in this life and in the next, there would be greater care and reflection in their decisions; they would pray more assiduously and show greater courage and logic in forestalling the causes of their spiritual and moral collapse.

87. Mother Church takes particular interest in what befalls young priests who, no matter how great the zeal and enthusiasm with which they entered the sacred ministry, have nevertheless been troubled later on in performing their duties by feelings of hopelessness, doubt, desire, or folly. Hence, especially in these circumstances, it is the wish of the Church that every persuasive means available be used to lead our brothers from this wavering state and restore to them peace of soul, trust, penance, and their former zeal. It is only when no other solution can be found for a priest in this unhappy condition that he should be relieved of his office.

88. There are some whose priesthood cannot be saved, but whose serious dispositions nevertheless give promise of their being able to live as good Christian lay people. To these the Holy See, having studied all the circumstances with their bishops or with their religious superiors, sometimes grants a dispensation, thus letting love conquer sorrow. In order, however, that her unhappy but always dear son may have a salutary sign of her maternal grief and a keener remembrance of the universal need of God's mercy, in these cases she imposes some works of piety and reparation.

89. Inspiring this discipline, which is at once severe and merciful, are justice and truth, prudence and reserve. It is without doubt a discipline which will confirm good priests in their determination to live lives of purity and holiness. At the same time it will be a warning to those aspiring to the priesthood. Guided by the wisdom of those who edu-

cate them, they will approach their priesthood fully aware of its obligations and entirely forgetfully of self, responding generously to divine grace and the will of Christ and His Church.

90. Finally, and with deep joy, We thank Our Lord because many priests who for a time had been unfaithful to their obligations have again, with the grace of the High Priest, found the path and given joy to all by becoming anew exemplary pastors. With admirable good will, they used all the means which were helpful to ensure their return, especially an intense life of prayer, humility, persevering effort sustained by regular reception of the Sacrament of Penance.

91. There is an irreplaceable and very effective means to ensure for our dear priests an easier and happier way of being faithful to their obligations, and it is one which they have the right and duty to find in you, venerable brother bishops. It was you who called them and destined them to be priests; it was you who placed your hands on their heads; with you they are one in sharing the honor of the priesthood by virtue of the Sacrament of Orders; it is you whom they make present in the community of the faithful; with you they are united in a spirit of trust and generosity since, in as far as is compatible with their order, they take upon themselves your duties and concerns.[137] In choosing a life dedicated to celibacy they follow the ancient examples of the prelates of the East and West; this provides a new motive for union between bishop and priest and a sound hope that they will live together more closely.

92. The love which Jesus had for His Apostles showed itself very clearly when He made them ministers of His real and Mystical Body;[138] and even you in whose person "Our

[137] Cf. LG, no. 28.
[138] Cf. Jn 13–17.

Lord Jesus Christ, the high priest, is present in the midst of those who believe," [139] know that you owe the best part of your hearts and pastoral care to your priests and to the young men preparing to be priests.[140] In no other way can you better show this conviction than in the conscious responsibility and sincere and unconquerable love with which you preside over the education of your seminarians, and help your priests in every way possible to remain faithful to their vocation and their duties.

93. Your fraternal and kindly presence must fill up in advance the human loneliness of the priest, which is so often the cause of his discouragement and temptations.[141] Before being the superiors and judges of your priests, be their teachers, fathers, friends, their good and kind brothers always ready to understand, to sympathize and to help. Encourage your priests in every possible way to be your personal friends and to be very open with you. This will not weaken the relationship of juridical obedience; rather it will transform it into pastoral love so that they will obey more willingly, sincerely and securely. If they have a filial trust in you, your priests will be able in time to open up their souls and to confide their difficulties in you in the certainty that they can rely on your kindness to be protected from eventual defeat, without a servile fear of punishment, but in the filial expectation of correction, pardon and help, which will inspire them to resume their difficult journey with a new confidence.

94. Venerable brothers, all of you are certainly convinced that to restore to the soul of a priest joy in and enthusiasm for his vocation, interior peace and salvation, is

[139] LG, no. 21.
[140] Cf. PO, no. 7.
[141] Cf. ibid.

an urgent and glorious ministry which has an incalculable influence on a multitude of souls. There will be times when you must exercise your authority by showing a just severity toward those few who, after having resisted your kindness, by their conduct cause scandal to the People of God; but you will take the necessary precautions to ensure their seeing the error of their ways. Following the example of Our Lord Jesus, "the Shepherd and Guardian of your souls," [142] do not crush the "bruised reed" nor quench the "smoldering wick"; [143] like Jesus, heal their wounds, [144] save what was lost; [145] with eagerness and love go in search of the lost sheep and bring him back to the warmth of the sheepfold [146] and like Him, try until the end [147] to call back the unfaithful friend.

95. We are certain, venerable brothers, that you will leave nothing undone to foster, by your teaching, prudence and pastoral zeal, the ideal of consecrated celibacy among your clergy. We are sure too that you will never neglect those priests who have strayed from the house of God, their true home, no matter where their painful odyssey has led them; for they still remain your sons.

96. Priestly virtue is a treasure that belongs to the whole Church. It is an enrichment and a splendor above the ordinary, which redounds to the building up and the profit of the entire People of God. We wish therefore to address to all the faithful, Our children in Christ, an affectionate and urgent exhortation. We wish that they too feel responsible

---

[142] 1 Pt 2:25.
[143] Mt 12:20.
[144] Cf. Lk 9:11.
[145] Cf. Mt 18:12.
[146] Cf. Lk 15:4ff.
[147] Cf. Lk 22:48.

for the virtue of those brothers of theirs who have undertaken the mission of serving them in the priesthood for the salvation of their souls. They should pray and work for priestly vocations; they should help priests wholeheartedly, with filial love and ready collaboration; they should have the firm intention of offering them the consolation of a joyous response to their pastoral labors. They should encourage these, their fathers in Christ, to overcome the difficulties of every sort which they encounter as they fulfill their duties, with entire faithfulness, to the edification of all. In a spirit of faith and Christian love, they should foster a deep respect and a delicate reserve in their dealings with priests, on account of their condition as men entirely consecrated to Christ and to the Church.

97. Our invitation goes out specially to those lay people who seek God with greater earnestness and intensity, and strive after Christian perfection while living in the midst of their fellow men. By their devoted and warm friendship they can be of great assistance to the Church's ministers since it is the laity, occupied with temporal affairs while at the same time aiming at a more generous and perfect conformity to their baptismal vocation, who are in a position, in many cases, to enlighten and encourage the priest. The integrity of his vocation, one that plunges him into the mystery of Christ and the Church, can suffer harm from various circumstances and from contamination by a destructive worldliness. In this way the whole People of God will honor Christ our Lord in those who represent Him and of whom He has said: "He who receives you receives me, and he who receives me receives him who sent me,"[148] promising an assured reward to anyone who in

[148] Mt 10:40.

any way shows charity toward those whom He has sent.[149]

98. Venerable brothers, pastors of God's flock throughout the world, and dearly beloved priests, Our sons and brothers: as We come to the end of this letter which We have addressed to you, We invite you, with a soul responsive to Christ's great love, to turn your eyes and heart with renewed confidence and filial hope to the most loving Mother of Jesus and Mother of the Church, and to invoke for the Catholic priesthood her powerful and maternal intercession. In her the People of God admire and venerate the image of the Church, and model of faith, charity and perfect union with Him. May Mary Virgin and Mother obtain for the Church, which also is hailed as virgin and mother[150] to rejoice always, though with due humility, in the faithfulness of her priests to the sublime gift of holy virginity they have received, and to see it flourishing and appreciated ever more and more in every walk of life, so that the army of those who "follow the divine Lamb wherever He goes"[151] may increase throughout the earth.

99. The Church proclaims her hope in Christ; she is conscious of the critical shortage of priests when compared with the spiritual necessities of the world's population; but she is confident in her expectation which is founded on the infinite and mysterious power of grace, that the high spiritual quality of her ministers will bring about an increase also in their numbers, for everything is possible to God.[152]

In this faith and in this hope, may the apostolic blessing

[149] Cf. Mt 10:42.
[150] Cf. LG, nos. 63–64.
[151] Ap 14:4.
[152] Cf. Mk 10:27; Lk 1:37.

which we impart with all Our heart be for all a pledge of heavenly graces and the testimony of Our fatherly affection.

Given at Rome, at St. Peter's, June 24, 1967,
the feast of St. John the Baptist,
in the fifth year of Our pontificate.

The Meaning of Celibacy

POPE JOHN PAUL II

Allow me at this point to touch upon the question of priestly celibacy. I shall deal with it summarily, because it has already been considered in a profound and complete way during the Council, and subsequently in the Encyclical *Sacerdotalis Cælibatus*, and again at the ordinary session of the 1971 Synod of Bishops. This reflection has shown itself to be necessary both in order to present the matter in a still more mature way, and also in order to explain even more deeply the meaning of the decision that the Latin Church took so many centuries ago and to which she has sought to be faithful, and desires to maintain this fidelity also in the future. The importance of the question under consideration is so great, and its link with the language of the Gospel itself so close, that in this case we cannot reason with categories different from those used by the Council, the Synod of Bishops and the great Pope Paul VI himself. We can only seek to understand this question more deeply and to respond to it more maturely, freeing ourselves from the various objections that have always—as happens today too—been raised against priestly celibacy, and also freeing ourselves from the different interpretations that appeal to criteria alien to the Gospel, to Tradition and to the Church's Magisterium—criteria, we would add, whose "anthropological" correctness and basis in fact are seen to be very dubious and of relative value.

Excerpted from the first Holy Thursday Letter to Priests (1979).

Nor must we be too surprised at all the objections and criticisms which have intensified during the postconciliar period, even though today in some places they seem to be growing less. Did not Jesus Christ, after He had presented the disciples with the question of the renunciation of marriage "for the sake of the kingdom of heaven," add these significant words: "Let anyone accept this who can"?[1] The Latin Church has wished, and continues to wish, referring to the example of Christ the Lord Himself, to the apostolic teaching and to the whole Tradition that is proper to her, that *all those who receive the Sacrament of Orders should embrace this renunciation "for the sake of the kingdom of heaven."* This tradition, however, is linked with respect for different traditions of other Churches. In fact, this tradition constitutes a characteristic, a peculiarity and a heritage of the Latin Catholic Church, a tradition to which she owes much and in which she is resolved to persevere, in spite of all the difficulties to which such fidelity could be exposed, and also in spite of the various symptoms of weakness and crisis in individual priests. We are all aware that "we have this treasure in earthen vessels"[2] yet we know very well that it is precisely a treasure.

Why is it a treasure? Do we wish thereby to reduce the value of marriage and the vocation to family life? Or are we succumbing to a Manichean contempt for the human body and its functions? Do we wish in some way to devalue love, which leads a man and a woman to marriage and the wedded unity of the body, thus forming "one flesh"?[3] How could we think and reason like that, if we know, believe and proclaim, following St. Paul, that marriage is a

[1] Mt 19:12.
[2] Cf. 2 Cor 4:7.
[3] Gen 2:24; cf. Mt 19:6.

"great mystery" in reference to Christ and the Church?[4] However, none of the reasons whereby people sometimes try to "convince us" of the inopportuneness of celibacy corresponds to the truth, the truth that the Church proclaims and seeks to realize in life through the commitment to which priests oblige themselves before ordination. The essential, proper and adequate reason, in fact, is contained in the truth that Christ declared when He spoke about the renunciation of marriage for the sake of the Kingdom of Heaven, and which St. Paul proclaimed when he wrote that each person in the Church has his or her own particular gifts.[5] Celibacy is precisely a "gift of the Spirit." A similar though different gift is fundamental for the building up of the great community of the Church, the People of God. But if this community wishes to respond fully to its vocation in Jesus Christ, there will also have to be realized in it, in the correct proportion, that other "gift," the gift of celibacy "for the sake of the kingdom of heaven."[6]

Why does the Latin Catholic Church link this gift not only with the life of those who accept the strict program of the evangelical counsels in Religious Institutes but also with the vocation to the hierarchical and ministerial priesthood? She does it because celibacy "for the sake of the kingdom" is not only an eschatological sign; it also has a great social meaning, in the present life, for the service of the People of God. Through his celibacy, the priest becomes the "man for others," in a different way from the man who, by binding himself in conjugal union with a woman, also becomes, as husband and father, a man "for others," especially in the radius of his own family: for his

[4] Cf. Eph 5:32.
[5] Cf. 1 Cor 7:7.
[6] Mt 19:12.

wife, and, together with her, for the children, to whom he gives life. The priest, by renouncing this fatherhood proper to married men, seeks another fatherhood and, as it were, even another motherhood, recalling the words of the Apostle about children whom he begets in suffering.[7] These are children of his spirit, people entrusted to his solicitude by the Good Shepherd. These people are many, more numerous than an ordinary human family can embrace. The pastoral vocation of priests is great, and the Council teaches that it is universal: It is directed towards the whole Church,[8] and therefore it is of a missionary character. Normally, it is linked to the service of a particular community of the People of God, in which each individual expects attention, care and love. The heart of the priest, in order that it may be available for this service, must be free. Celibacy is a sign of a freedom that exists for the sake of service. According to this sign, the hierarchical or "ministerial" priesthood is, according to the tradition of our Church, more strictly "ordered" to the common priesthood of the faithful.

[7] Cf. 1 Cor 4:15; Gal 4:19.
[8] Cf. *Presbyterorum Ordinis*, 3, 6, 10, 12.

DR. JOHN M. HAAS is the President of the National Catholic Bioethics Center in Boston, Massachusetts. He received his Ph.D. in Moral Theology from the Catholic University of America and his S.T.L. in Moral Theology from the University of Fribourg, Switzerland. He has taught at Saint Charles Borromeo Seminary in Philadelphia, the Pontifical John Paul II Institute for Studies in Marriage and the Family in Washington, D.C., Ohio State University, and the Pontifical College Josephinum in Worthington, Ohio. He is the editor of and a contributor to *Crisis in Conscience* and a contributing editor to *Crisis* and *Touchstone* magazines. His opinion pieces have appeared in *The New York Times*, *The Boston Globe*, and *The Philadelphia Inquirer*. He has lectured extensively in the United States and abroad. Dr. Haas and his wife, Martha, are the parents of nine children and reside in Philadelphia.

DR. DAVID HARTMAN is senior minister of First Christian Church (Disciples of Christ) in Wichita Falls, Texas. An ordained minister for 22 years, he is a graduate of Vanderbilt Divinity School and Lexington Theological Seminary. He and his wife, Jessica, have three children.

MRS. JESSICA HARTMAN is the mother of three children, a school teacher, and a church organist. She has recently moved from Harrodsburg, Kentucky, to teach religion and chemistry at Notre Dame High School in Wichita Falls, Texas. She graduated with a bachelor of science from the University of Kentucky and earned her master of arts in education at the College of William and Mary.

KENNETH J. HOWELL is the director of the John Henry Newman Institute of Catholic Thought, and Adjunct Associate Professor of Religious Studies at the University of Illinois, Champaign–Urbana. He teaches courses on Catholicism and conducts research in the history of science and religion. He is author of

God's Two Books: Copernican Cosmology and Biblical Interpretation in Early Modern Science (University of Notre Dame Press), and *Mary of Nazareth: Sign and Instrument of Christian Unity* (Queenship Publishing). After eighteen years of Presbyterian ministry and teaching in a theological seminary, Mr. Howell entered the Catholic Church in 1996.

DR. WANDA POLTAWSKA is Professor of Pastoral Medicine at the Pontifical Academy of Cracow. She is a member of the Pontifical Council for the Family, a consultant to the Pontifical Council for Health Care Workers, and a member of the Pontifical Academy for Life.

REV. PETER M. J. STRAVINSKAS is the founding editor of *The Catholic Answer* magazine, published by Our Sunday Visitor, Inc. He is the author of more than twenty books and five hundred articles. He holds degrees in Classical Languages and French, biblical theology, and school administration from Seton Hall University and Immaculate Conception Seminary, as well as a licentiate in systematic theology from the Pontifical Faculty of the Immaculate Conception in Washington, D.C., a doctorate in education from Fordham University, and a doctorate in theology from the University of Dayton and the Marianum in Rome.

He serves as adjunct professor of education at Seton Hall University in South Orange, New Jersey; adjunct professor of education and classics at Holy Apostles Seminary in Cromwell, Connecticut; and adjunct professor of humanities in the Casperson Graduate School of Drew University in Madison, New Jersey. He has conducted retreats and lectured in seventy dioceses of the United States and more than a dozen abroad.